**Leon Dallin**

*California State College at Long Beach*

# Introduction to Music Reading

## A PROGRAM FOR PERSONAL INSTRUCTION

*A Crescendo Book*
*TAPLINGER PUBLISHING COMPANY*
*New York*

First Taplinger/Crescendo Printing
Published in 1982 by
TAPLINGER PUBLISHING CO., INC.
New York, New York

Library of Congress Catalog Card No. 66-19139
ISBN 0-8008-4201-4

From "The Japanese Sandman," page 38: Copyright 1920 by Jerome H. Remick & Company. Copyright renewed and assigned to Remick Music Corporation. Used by permission.

From "While We Danced at the Mardi Gras," page 32: Copyright 1931 by the Miller Music Corporation.

# preface

You can learn to read music. This book utilizes a recently developed method of self-instruction to teach music reading quickly and efficiently. After a few hours of study you will be able to read music notation, to pick out simple melodies on the piano, to follow printed music as it is played, and to use the basic terminology in talking and writing about music.

Whatever your interest in music, the first step is to learn music notation. Otherwise, your participation in music is limited to the few songs you can learn by rote or play by ear. Without knowing notation, you cannot read the examples of music in appreciation texts, in program notes, or on record jackets. Courses in music either begin with music reading or presuppose this ability. The approach of this book is equally effective for students whose goal is to sing, play, listen, or teach.

This is a programed book. Its format is significantly different from that of a conventional text. Small units of information are presented in a carefully ordered sequence. At each step you are asked to fill in a blank, answer a question, or perform an exercise. This keeps you alert and actively engaged in the learning process. You are rewarded by a sense of achievement, and learning is reinforced when your response agrees with the one printed in the book for immediate comparison. The design of the program assures correct responses most of the time. Faulty responses are corrected before misconceptions develop. Revolutionary as this approach may appear, it is based upon principles as old as the student-teacher relationship. Only its application in book form is new.

A programed book has several advantages. It is a medium of instruction complete in itself, not dependent upon a teacher or a teaching machine. You study at your convenience and proceed at your own pace, rapidly through material you find easy and deliberately through material you find more demanding. This programed text expedites learning to sing and play and serves as a point of departure for intelligent listening. It supplements conventional texts and music methods, and classroom or private instruction.

*Introduction to Music Reading* provides a solid foundation for the study of music. To discover how this is accomplished, turn to the Study Instructions.

# study
# instructions

This is a programed text to be studied, not a book to be read. The Preface tells you some of the things to expect in a programed text. These instructions tell you how to study this particular program.

First, tear off the perforated card inside the front cover. This *masking card* is to be placed just below each line of words or music and moved down the page as you read. In each blank space like this, _____, you are to write the missing word, number, or symbol. When the response involves music notation, the line is below the staff and may extend the full width of the example or of the page. You may need to refer to preceding statements, to the previous example, or to the keyboard diagram before responding. Always write your response above the line before sliding the masking card down to reveal the correct response printed directly below.

Compare your response with the correct response immediately. Synonyms and numbers or symbols with essentially the same meaning are acceptable. When your response and the one given do not agree, draw a line through your answer and copy the correct one in the margin. Refer back to the explanatory material and determine the reason for your error.

Since music reading involves skill as well as knowledge, you are frequently directed to perform a rhythm or a melody. The rhythms and melodies are taken from familiar music to enable you to judge for yourself whether or not your performance of the exercise is correct. In some examples the song title is below the music so that you will read the notation and not perform the song from memory. The amount of emphasis on performance will depend upon your special interest in music and the degree of proficiency you wish to attain.

An index is provided for your convenience in looking up specific words and topics. The answers corrected in the margin help you locate potential trouble spots for review.

Turn the page and begin your *Introduction to Music Reading*.

# rhythm

Imagine that you are walking at a comfortable pace. Now clap your hands with each imaginary step. Clapping at equal time intervals establishes a regular pulse. The sound of music also establishes a regular _____. Whenever you march, dance, or tap your toe to music, you are

PULSE

responding to music's regular _____.

PULSE

The regular pulse in music is called the *beat*. Various symbols are used to represent the _____. One of the symbols for a beat looks like this:

BEAT

♩

The symbols which represent beats, and all durations in music, are *notes*. Most notes have fractional names like *half note, quarter note, eighth note,* etc. The symbol shown for a beat is a *quarter note*. This ♩ is a _____ _____.

QUARTER         NOTE

Quarter note    ♩

Write a line of quarter notes.

♩ ♩ ♩ ♩ ♩ ♩ ♩ ♩ ♩ ♩ ♩ ♩ ♩ ♩ ♩ ♩

Imagine now that you are walking and taking a step with each beat. The beats, coming alternately with the left foot and the right foot, are grouped in pairs.

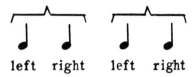

left    right    left    right

In marching it is customary to start with the left foot on a *strong beat* of the music, that is, on a beat which is stressed or *accented*. The right foot follows on a weaker beat, a beat which is not stressed or _____. The alternating strong and weak _____ produce a recurrent strong-weak or accented-unaccented pattern.

ACCENTED                                                    BEATS

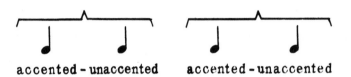

accented - unaccented    accented - unaccented

One of the basic rhythms of music is produced by alternating accented and unaccented beats of equal duration. The alternating accents divide the beats into groups of _____.

TWO

The first beat of each group is accented, and the second is _____.

UNACCENTED

Patterns of accented and unaccented beats form *measures*. The simplest measures have a two-beat pattern in which the first beat is accented and the second beat is _____. Patterns of accented and unaccented beats form rhythmic units known as _____.

UNACCENTED

MEASURES

Measures of music are divided by *bar lines*. A bar _____ denotes the end of one measure and the beginning of the next _____. Identical beat patterns occur between _____ lines.

LINE

MEASURE

BAR

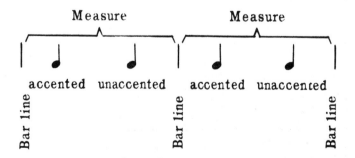

Measure         Measure

accented  unaccented    accented  unaccented

Bar line    Bar line    Bar line

The beats within measures are numbered consecutively. The first beat following a bar line is numbered 1. The second beat following a bar line is numbered _____, etc.

2

Write the numbers for the beats below the notes in each measure.

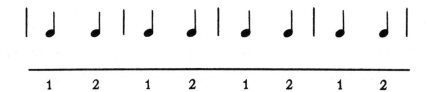

1   2   1   2   1   2   1   2

Measures always begin with an accented beat and end with an unaccented beat. In two-beat measures the first beat is _____, and the second beat is _____.

ACCENTED          UNACCENTED

Bar lines precede accented beats and follow _____ beats.

UNACCENTED

Draw bar lines between the measures and underline the numbers of accented beats.

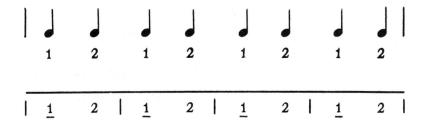

Write two quarter notes in each measure, above the numbers.

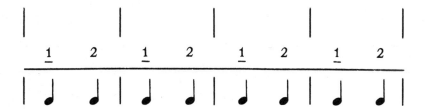

Clap the rhythm you have just written. The beats should be spaced evenly. Clap louder for the accented first beats and softer for the unaccented second beats.

Continue clapping and count *ONE, two, ONE, two.* Say the number at the exact instant the clap sounds, and be sure that the *ONE* coincides with the louder clapping sound.

✠ ✠ ✠ ✠

At the beginning of each piece of music there are two numbers, one above the other. These two numbers are the *time signature,* also called the *meter signature. Time signature* will be used in this book, though the rhythm pattern indicated by the time signature will be called the *meter.* The lower number of the time _____ shows which note symbol is used to represent the
<small>SIGNATURE</small>
beat. In all previous examples the beat has been represented by a _____ note. When
<small>QUARTER</small>
the beat is represented by a quarter note, the lower number in the time signature is 4. When the lower number in the time signature is 4, the beat is represented by a _____ _____.
<small>QUARTER</small>   <small>NOTE</small>
The upper number in the _____ _____ shows the number of
<small>TIME</small>   <small>SIGNATURE</small>
beats in a measure. If there are two beats in a measure, the upper number is _____.
<small>2</small>
When the upper number is 2, there are _____ beats in a measure. Measures of two
<small>TWO</small>
quarter-note beats have a time signature like this:

$$\text{Two} \rightarrow \mathbf{\frac{2}{4}} \quad \text{♩} \quad \text{♩} \mid$$
Quarter notes ⟶

The number of beats in a measure is indicated by the _____ number of the
<small>UPPER</small>
time signature. The kind of note used to represent the beat is indicated by the _____
<small>LOWER</small>
number of the time signature.

Time signatures are expressed verbally by saying the two numbers in succession, the upper number first. Thus the time signature $\frac{2}{4}$ (for convenience, henceforth written in the text 2/4) is called *two-four,* and music which has this time signature is in _____ time.
<small>TWO-FOUR</small>
Music in 2/4 _____ has a two-beat rhythmic pattern, and the beats are represented
<small>TIME</small>
by_____ _____. The first beat in each measure is accented, and the second
<small>QUARTER</small>   <small>NOTES</small>
beat is _____. The measures are divided by _____ _____.
<small>UNACCENTED</small>   <small>BAR</small>   <small>LINES</small>
The end of an exercise or a composition is marked by a *double bar.* A double _____
<small>BAR</small>
consists of two adjacent bar lines, the second of which is slightly heavier than the first. At the end of the next exercise there is a double bar. The exercise is in 2/4 time. Count and clap the rhythm.

The addition of two dots beside a double bar makes a *repeat sign.*

Repeat signs      ‖:                       :‖

Two repeat signs, one with the dots on the right side of the double bar and the other with the dots on the left side of the double bar, indicate that the passage between them is to be repeated, that is, performed twice. The repetition is made without stopping and without interrupting the regular pulse of the beat. If only the repeat sign with the dots on the left appears, the exercise or composition is to be repeated from the beginning.

Make the necessary additions to the double bars to show that the passage between them is to be repeated.

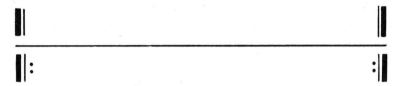

Clap the rhythm of the following exercise as you have in previous ones, but sing *loo* in place of counting.

The sign at the end of the exercise is a _____ sign. Did you perform the exer-
REPEAT
cise twice before stopping? If not, return to the exercise and perform it again, this time observing the repeat sign.

        ✠     ✠     ✠     ✠

For every note, indicating sound, there is an equivalent *rest*, indicating silence.

Quarter note     ♩        Quarter rest     𝄽

To notate silence equal to a quarter note, a quarter _____ is written. Quarter rests
REST
substitute for quarter notes whenever silence is required. For example, quarter rests may substitute for quarter notes in measures of 2/4 time.

Clap a regular background beat and sing the following exercises containing rests. Sustain the sound of the syllable *loo* for precisely the duration of one beat where notes are written, and remain silent an equivalent time interval where rests (r) are written. Repeat each exercise.

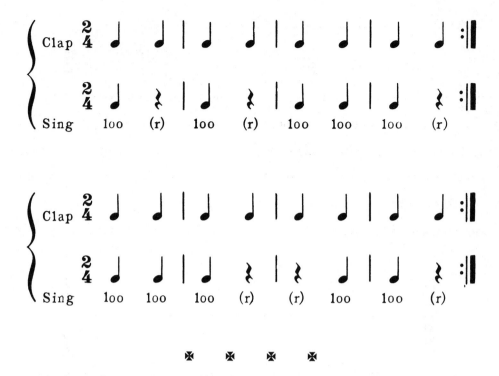

✠ ✠ ✠ ✠

*Rhythmic value* is the expression used to describe the *relative duration* of notes and rests. Since relative duration is the basis for naming notes and rests, the names define fixed rhythmic relationships between the various symbols. The beat, within a given context, provides a constant time unit which serves as a point of reference for longer and shorter durations.

When the beat is represented by a quarter note, a note with a rhythmic value of two beats is a *half note*. A half note is shaped like a quarter note, but the head is open.

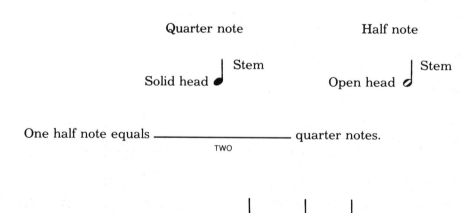

One half note equals _____ quarter notes.
TWO

A half note is twice as long as a ———————— note. A quarter note is half as long as a
<br>QUARTER

———————— note. The rhythmic value of two quarter notes can be represented by one
<br>HALF

———————— note. In measures of 2/4 time there may be two ———————— notes
<br>HALF                                     QUARTER

or one ———————— note.
<br>HALF

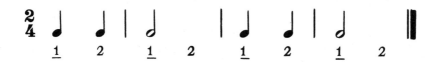

<br>1     2     1     2     1     2     1     2

In 2/4 time each quarter note receives ———————— count. Each half note receives
<br>ONE

———————— counts.
<br>TWO

Write the counts under the notes.

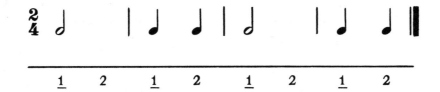

<br>1     2     1     2     1     2     1     2

Beats have been counted and clapped in previous exercises. Another way to mark the beat is by tapping with the toe or heel. Maintaining the beat by tapping leaves the voice free to sing and the hands free to clap other rhythms or play an instrument. Perform the next exercise in the following ways:

1. Establish the quarter-note beat by counting and/or tapping with the toe or heel at a moderate speed.

2. Continue counting and/or tapping the beats and clap the half notes.

3. Maintain the beat by tapping and sing half notes using a neutral syllable such as *loo*. Sustain the sound for the full value of the notes.

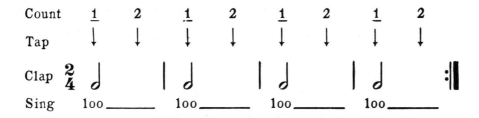

The following rhythm patterns contain quarter and half notes in various combinations. Perform them in the ways suggested for the previous exercise. Similar procedures should be employed in practicing all subsequent rhythm studies.

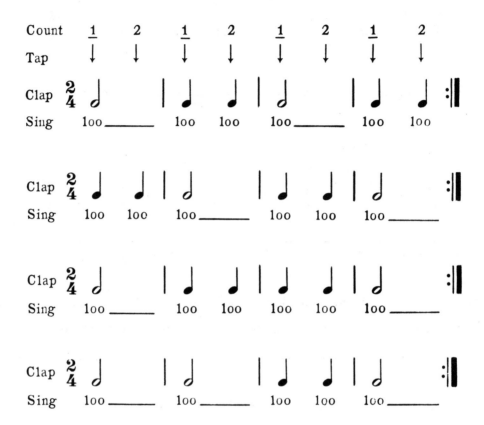

Now perform the four rhythm patterns in succession without stopping or repeating. The beat may be either fast or slow, but once established it must remain constant throughout. If you make a mistake, start over with a slower beat. If you do it perfectly the first time, increase the *tempo* (i.e., establish a faster beat) and do it again. The *relative* duration of notes is unaffected by changes in the speed.

The following rhythm using quarter and half notes in 2/4 time is from a familiar song. Perform the rhythm and see if you can recognize the song from its rhythm alone. The important thing is to perform the rhythm correctly. Identifying the song is incidental.

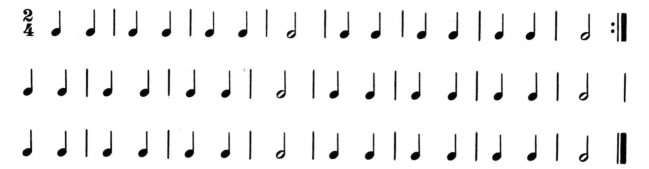

Name of song _____

TWINKLE, TWINKLE, LITTLE STAR

Now sing the song with the words.

Twinkle, twinkle, little star, how I wonder what you are,
Up above the world so high, like a diamond in the sky.
When the evening sun is set, and the grass with dew is wet,
Then I see your little light; twinkle, twinkle, all the night.

Did you perform the rhythm correctly? If not, try it again, following the notation and associating the rhythmic relationships with the symbols.

The rest equivalent of a half note is a half _____. A half rest is an oblong mark

REST

above a line, a segment of which is shown with the half-rest symbol.

Half note ♩            Half rest ▬

Write the symbols indicated.

Quarter note _____         Half note _____

Quarter rest _____         Half rest _____

In 2/4 time a half rest indicates _____ beats or counts of silence. The next exer-

TWO

cise contains all of the note and rest symbols introduced thus far. Write the counts under the symbols and perform the rhythm, being careful to maintain the beat during the silences.

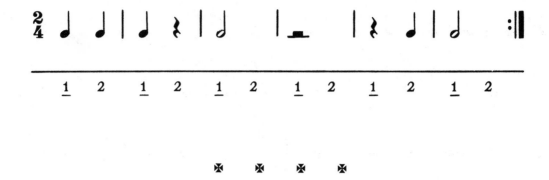

1   2   1   2   1   2   1   2   1   2   1   2

✠   ✠   ✠   ✠

Two-beat patterns like the one found in 2/4 time are often combined in a single measure. Each measure then has four quarter-note beats, and the time signature is 4/4. The lower number of the time signature is 4, indicating that the beat is represented by a _____ _____.
QUARTER          NOTE
The upper number of the time signature is also 4, showing that there are four beats in a _____.
MEASURE

Four → **4**<br>Quarter notes → **4**  ♩  ♩  ♩  ♩ |

The pattern of accents in one measure of 4/4 time is similar to that in two measures of 2/4 time.

**2/4**  ♩  ♩ | ♩  ♩ |
1   2   1   2

**4/4**  ♩  ♩  ♩  ♩ |
1   2   3   4

In 4/4 time, accents come on the first and _____ beats. The second and fourth
THIRD
beats are _____.
UNACCENTED
The first beat in a 4/4 measure receives a *primary accent* and the third beat a lesser *secondary accent*. Therefore, a measure of 4/4 time is not quite the same as two measures of 2/4. Write the counts under the notes of the following measures in 4/4 time and underline the numbers of accented beats, both primary and secondary.

| 1 | 2 | 3 | 4 | 1 | 2 | 3 | 4 | 1 | 2 | 3 | 4 | 1 | 2 | 3 | 4 |

The note and rest symbols used in 2/4 time are also used in 4/4 time, and their relationships are unchanged. The following rhythm occurs four times in succession in a familiar song. Count or tap a background beat and clap or sing the rhythm the required number of times. Always perform the rhythm, and name the song if you can, before looking at the title.

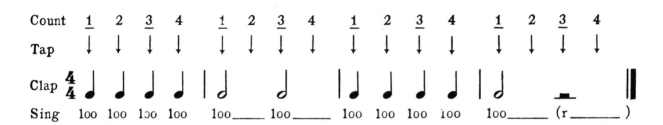

Name of song _____

AU CLAIR DE LA LUNE
(In the Shining Moonlight)

A note which is twice as long as a half note and four times as long as a quarter note is a *whole note*. The symbol for a _____ WHOLE _____ note is an open oval without a stem.

Whole note  𝐨

One whole note equals two _____ HALF _____ notes.

𝐨 = 𝅗𝅥 𝅗𝅥

One half note equals two _____ QUARTER _____ notes.

𝅗𝅥 = ♩ ♩

One whole note equals four _____ notes.
QUARTER

When the beat is represented by a quarter note, as it is in 4/4 time, a whole note receives four counts. One whole note fills a complete measure in 4/4 _____.
TIME

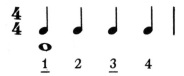

The following rhythm uses whole notes in 4/4 time. Perform the rhythm, and name the song if you can, before associating the rhythm with the words.

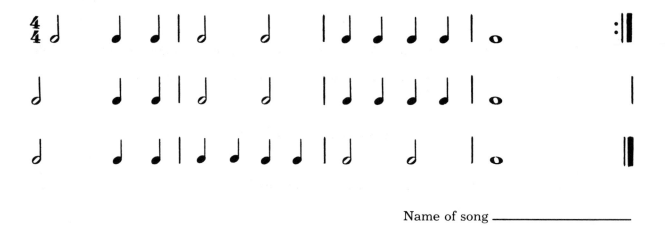

Name of song _____
ABIDE WITH ME

Abide with me, fast falls the eventide;
The darkness deepens, Lord, with me abide.
When other helpers fail and comforts flee,
Help of the helpless, O abide with me.

The symbol **C** may be used in place of a 4/4 time signature for measures of four quarter-note beats. When the symbol is used in place of the numbers, it is customary to refer to the time as *common time.* The symbol is a remnant from an almost obsolete set of time signatures, not an abbreviation for "common," but the similarity of the symbol and the letter *C* may serve as a memory aid.

Four - four time $\frac{4}{4}$ ♩ ♩ ♩ ♩ |

Common time C   1   2   3   4

Four-four time and common time signatures are completely interchangeable. The following song is written in common time. It could have been written in 4/4 time, just as any song in 4/4 time could be written in common time. Neither the notation nor the interpretation would be altered.

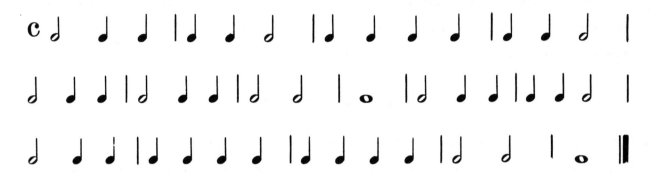

Name of song _____

FAIREST LORD JESUS
(Crusaders' Hymn)

Fair are the mead — ows,* fairer still the wood — lands,
Robed in the blooming — garb of spring; Jesus is fair — er,
Jesus is pur — er, Who makes the woeful heart to sing.

[*Note: A dash indicates that two notes of the melody come with the preceding word or syllable.]
Write two different time signatures appropriate for measures of four quarter notes.

Common time ___  C
                    ♩ ♩ ♩ ♩ |
Four-four time ___     1  2  3  4
                    $\frac{4}{4}$

A *whole rest* has the same shape as a half rest, but a whole rest is *below* a line. To be distinguished, whole- and half-rest symbols must be shown either above or below a line. In relation to the line, a half rest is _____ABOVE_____ the line, and a whole rest is _____BELOW_____ the line.

The rest with the greater value hangs down from the line.

Half rest     ▬

Whole rest     ▬

Tap a background beat and sing the following rhythm. Be silent where counts are shown in parentheses below the rests.

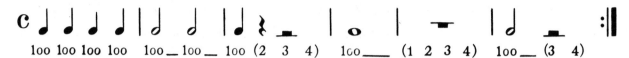

loo loo loo loo    loo __ loo __ loo (2   3   4)   loo ____ (1   2   3   4)   loo __ (3   4)

The rest symbol written above a line is a _____ rest. In 2/4 time or 4/4 time a half rest

HALF

receives _____ counts. The rest symbol written below a line is a _____ rest.

TWO                                                  WHOLE

In 4/4 time and common time a whole rest receives _____ counts.

FOUR

✠     ✠     ✠     ✠

A curved line connecting two notes of the same pitch is a *tie*. A _____ joins

TIE

two notes together and combines their rhythmic values. For example, a quarter note tied to another

quarter note is the equivalent of a _____ note.

HALF

$$\text{♩} \smile \text{♩} = \text{♩}$$

Tie ↗

A half note tied to another half note is the equivalent of a _____ note. Complete

WHOLE

the equation:

$$\text{♩} \smile \text{♩} = \underset{𝅝}{\phantom{x}}$$

Ties are used when a rhythmic value extends over a bar line or for some other reason cannot be written conveniently as one note. The next exercise shows a typical function of ties—joining notes of different measures across a bar line. Provide a background beat and sing the rhythm.

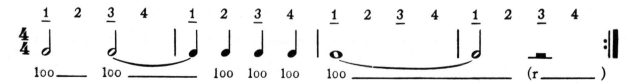

loo___    loo _____    loo loo loo   loo _____    (r _____ )

Ties are also used within measures. The following rhythm, which has values equal to three quarter notes, can be written with ties. Sing the rhythm while tapping or clapping the beat.

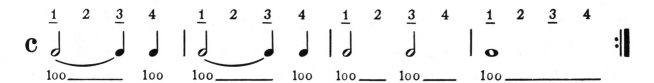

While this notation is possible, it is not usual. The usual symbol for a three-quarter value is a *dotted half note*.

One dotted half note   ♩. = ♩ ♩ ♩   Three quarter notes

A dot, like that shown, by the head of any note increases the value of the note by one half. Half the value of a half note is a quarter. A quarter added to a half gives a total value of three quarters.

$$\text{♩} = \text{♩} + \text{♩}$$
$$\text{♩.} = \text{♩} + \text{♩}$$

Stated another way, a dot adds the equivalent of the next shorter value to a note. After a half note, the next shorter value is a _____ note. A half note plus a quarter note equals
QUARTER
a _____ half note.
DOTTED

$$\text{♩} + \text{♩} = \text{♩.}$$

Dotted half notes eliminate the necessity for ties in notating the rhythm of the previous exercise. Both methods of notation are shown below for comparison. The second, without ties, is the customary notation for this rhythm.

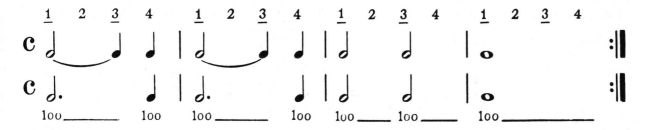

Practice the next rhythm, which has dotted half notes both beginning and ending measures, preparatory to the song which follows.

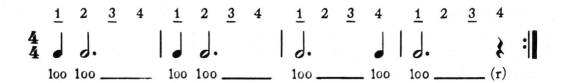

loo loo _____ loo loo _____ loo _____ loo loo _____ (r)

There are several dotted half notes in the next song. Sing its rhythm with *loo* and then verify the accuracy of your performance by singing the words and melody.

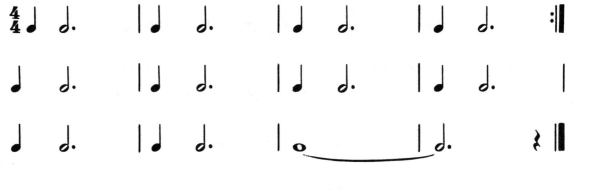

Name of song _____
JACOB'S LADDER

We are climbing Jacob's ladder,
We are climbing Jacob's ladder,
We are climbing Jacob's ladder,
Soldiers of the cross.

Dots added to rests have the same effect as dots added to notes, but dotted rests are not common.

$$\text{♩.} \quad = \quad \text{▬·} \quad (\text{rare})$$

The rest equivalent of a dotted half note is usually written with a half rest and a quarter rest, the order depending upon the location in the measure. Half rests as a rule start on an accented beat. This principle is observed in the following example where half rests are introduced on the first and third beats of the 4/4 measures.

1   2   3   4   1   2   3   4

In the time signatures introduced thus far (2/4, 4/4 and **C**) the beats are grouped in pairs. Each accented beat is followed by *one* _____ beat.

UNACCENTED

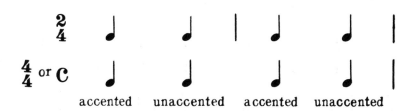

accented   unaccented   accented   unaccented

This is one of the two basic beat patterns.

The other basic beat pattern has *three beats*. The first beat is accented, as always, and the other two beats are unaccented. Each accented beat is followed by *two* _____ beats.

UNACCENTED

Clap a three-beat pattern accenting the first beat of each group. Count *ONE, two, three, ONE, two, three* as you clap. This is the beat pattern of waltzes.

A three-beat pattern can be written with three quarter notes in a measure. Add bar lines to the example and underline the numbers of accented beats.

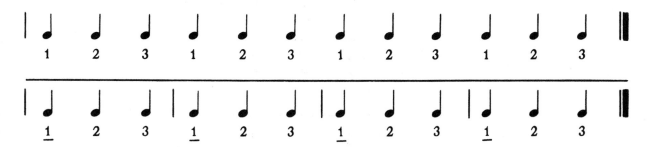

When measures consist of three quarter-note beats, the time signature is 3/4. The lower number, 4, indicates that the beats are represented by _____ notes. The upper number,

QUARTER

3, indicates that there are three beats in a _____.

MEASURE

Write quarter notes above the numbers to fill the measures of 3/4 time.

18

Music written in 3/4 time has a three-beat rhythmic pattern, and the beats are represented by

_____ notes. The first beat in each measure is accented, and the second and third
QUARTER

beats are _____.
UNACCENTED

Perform the following 3/4 rhythm in the ways suggested previously.

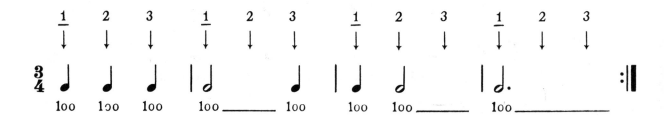

Observe that each measure of the previous exercise has a different rhythmic pattern. Write the

pattern of each measure in the space provided. Align the notes under the numbers of the beats.

| Measure | Pattern | | |
|---------|---|---|---|
| | 1 | 2 | 3 (beats) |
| 1. | ♩ | ♩ | ♩ |
| 2. | ♩ | | ♩ |
| 3. | ♩ | ♩ | |
| 4. | ♩. | | |

All four of these patterns, plus rests and ties, are used in the next song. Practice the rhythms

in various ways and then sing the melody — with the words if you know them, with *loo* if you do not.

Name of song _____

THE SIDEWALKS OF NEW YORK
(East Side, West Side)

✠  ✠  ✠  ✠

A piece may begin with one or more notes before the first primary accent. Notes preceding the first primary accent are *pickup notes* or *upbeats*. A measure containing pickup notes, also known as _____, is incomplete, that is, it has fewer beats than the number indicated in the
UPBEATS
time _____. When there is an incomplete measure at the beginning of a piece, there
SIGNATURE
is a complementary incomplete measure at the end of the piece. The time values of the two incomplete measures together equal one complete measure. In the incomplete measures the accents occur and the beats are numbered as if the incomplete last measure came before the pickup notes. The next two examples illustrate these principles.

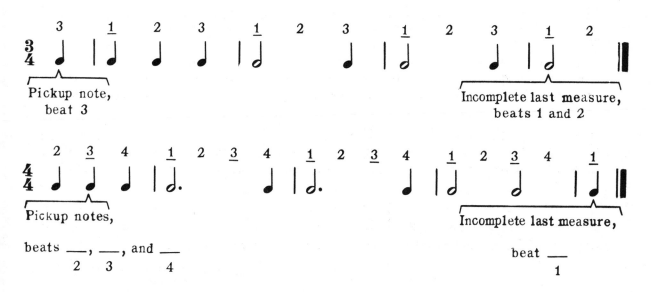

A song which begins with an unaccented syllable in the words normally begins with a pickup note in the music. Sing the next song, which illustrates this characteristic, correlating the accents in the words with those in the music.

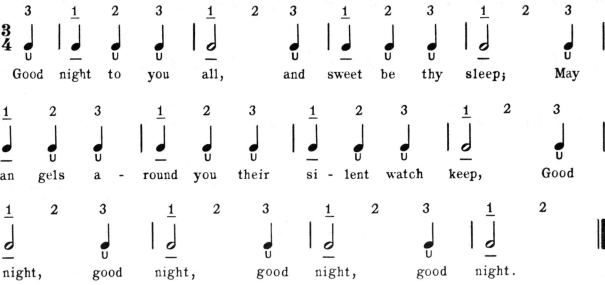

_____ Good Night

Observe how the accents in the words coincide with the accents in the music. The first word, which is unaccented, comes on an unaccented _____ of the measure. The last word,

BEAT

which is accented, begins on the first beat of the measure and receives a primary _____.

ACCENT

The pickup note occupies one beat, and the last (incomplete) measure has _____ beats

TWO

for a total of three beats in 3/4 time.

The next song illustrates the use of pickup notes in common (4/4) time. Clap the rhythm at a brisk pace and sing the words, exaggerating the accent on words which coincide with primary accents in the music.

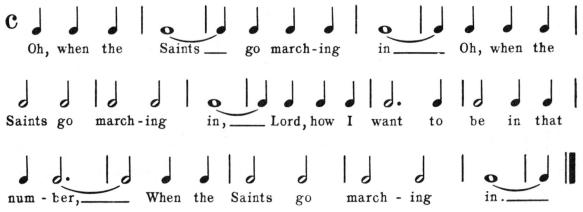

_____ When the Saints Go Marching In

⚜ ⚜ ⚜ ⚜

If you sang the previous song at the usual tempo (literally *time*, but meaning *rate of speed* in music), the quarter-note beats were very fast, so fast that you may have been inclined to count and feel *two* quarter notes in a beat. This not only is possible but preferable in songs like this.

When there are two quarter notes in a beat, the beat is represented by a half note, and the lower number of the time signature is _____. When there are two half-note beats in a measure, the upper number in the time signature is also _____.

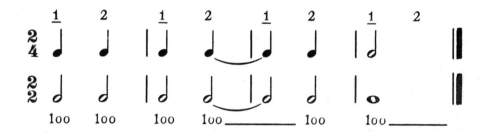

Since different note symbols can be used to represent the beat, the same rhythm can be notated in more than one way. The following rhythms look different but sound the same. Perform them looking first at one notation and then the other. The numbers and syllables apply to both versions.

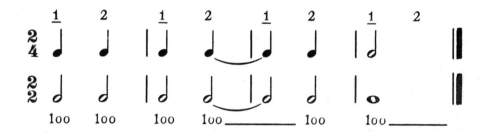

The *relative* duration of notes is not affected by the time signature. One half note equals two _____ notes in any time signature. When a half note represents the beat, a quarter note is only a half beat. In counting half beats say the syllable *and*, which will be represented by the symbol "&." In tapping, lift the heel or toe precisely on the half beat, dividing the beat equally. Count, tap, clap, and sing in various combinations the following rhythm.

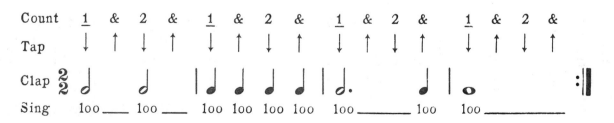

Count and tap half beats wherever it helps to clarify the rhythm. Dividing the beat will be necessary only occasionally after a feeling for equal division of the beat has been developed.

Measures of two half-note beats are indicated by a 2/2 time signature and also by this symbol: ¢ . Compare the symbol for 2/2 time with the one for 4/4 time.

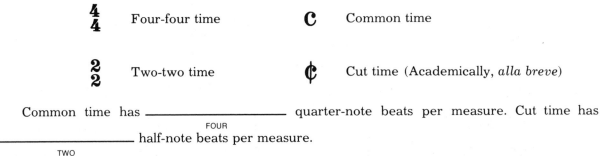

The symbols and the number time signatures are used interchangeably, but in speaking it is customary to distinguish between them as follows:

|   |   |   |   |
|---|---|---|---|
| $\frac{4}{4}$ | Four-four time | C | Common time |
| $\frac{2}{2}$ | Two-two time | ¢ | Cut time (Academically, *alla breve*) |

Common time has _____ FOUR _____ quarter-note beats per measure. Cut time has _____ TWO _____ half-note beats per measure.

Measures in four-four time, common time, two-two time, and cut time all have the same number of quarter notes: _____ FOUR _____. Any one of these time signatures could be used with the rhythmic notation of *When the Saints Go Marching In*. The relative durations would be the same, but the tapping and counting would be different, as shown.

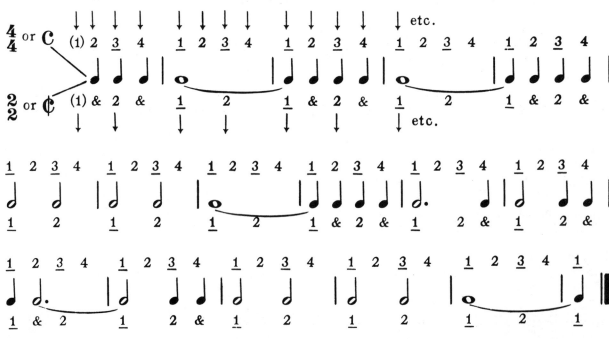

_____ When the Saints Go Marching In

Sing the rhythm of the melody while tapping the background beat for 4/4 and common time. Clap the rhythm of the melody while counting quarter-note beats. Repeat the process substituting the background beat of 2/2 and cut time and counting half-note beats. The slower, half-note beats probably seem more natural. This song is usually written in cut time.

Two of the basic three-beat patterns are combined in measures of six beats. When there are six beats in a measure, the upper number of the time signature is ——————————. When the beat is represented by a quarter note, the lower number of the time signature is ——————————. When there are six quarter-note beats in a measure, the time signature is ——————————. One measure of 6/4 time is the equivalent of two measures of 3/4 time.

6

4

6/4

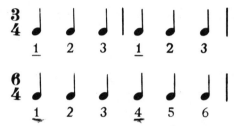

The six beats in 6/4 time divide into *two* groups of *three*, never into three groups of two. The primary accent falls on the —————————— beat of the measure, and the secondary accent falls on the —————————— beat of the measure. The unaccented beats in order are the second, ——————————, ——————————, and ——————————.

FIRST

FOURTH

THIRD    FIFTH    SIXTH

Perform the rhythm of the next song in a variety of ways making an audible difference between the primary and the secondary accents.

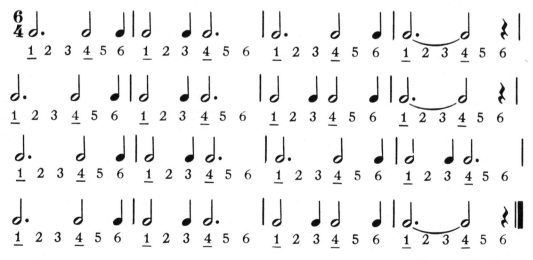

—— Nearer, My God, to Thee

Nearer, my God, to Thee! Nearer to Thee.
E'en tho' it be a cross, That — raiseth me,
Still all my song shall be, Nearer, my God, to Thee,
Nearer, my God, to Thee, Nearer to Thee.

To fill a full measure in 6/4 time with a single note, a new symbol is required — a *dotted whole note*. A dotted whole note equals two dotted half notes or six _____ notes.

QUARTER

Dotted whole note   𝅝· = 𝅗𝅥·   𝅗𝅥·

𝅝· = ♩ ♩ ♩ ♩ ♩ ♩

In the next exercise the dotted whole note comes at the end, where it is most apt to appear.

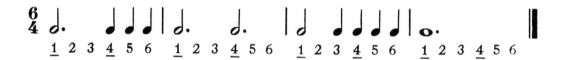

$\frac{6}{4}$ 𝅗𝅥·  ♩♩♩|𝅗𝅥·  𝅗𝅥·  |𝅗𝅥 ♩♩♩♩|𝅝·  ‖
    1 2 3 4 5 6  1 2 3 4 5 6  1 2 3 4 5 6  1 2 3 4 5 6

Theoretically the rest equivalent of a dotted whole note is a dotted whole rest. In practice a simple whole rest is used to denote full measures of silence in any meter.

✠   ✠   ✠   ✠

When there are six beats in a measure, a more usual symbol for the beat than a quarter note is an *eighth note*. Eighth notes look like this:

Eighth notes   ♪ ♪ ♪   or   ♫♫

The symbol for an individual eighth note is like the symbol for a quarter note with a *flag* attached to the *stem*.

Quarter note   Stem →  Head →  ♩   Eighth note   Stem →  Head →  ♪ ← Flag

The *head* and *stem* are the same for both quarter notes and _____ notes. Eighth

EIGHTH

notes have, in addition, a _____ attached to the stem.

FLAG

Write the symbols indicated.

Whole note ———————————— Half note ————————————

Quarter note ———————————— Eighth note ————————————

Groups of eighth notes are joined by *beams* which take the place of the flags on single eighth notes. The most usual groups consist of two, three, or four eighth notes.

Add beams to the symbols to make eighth notes as follows:

a. Six groups of two

b. Four groups of three

c. Three groups of four

Flags are used on individual eighth notes and in vocal music when each eighth note comes with a different word or syllable of the text. Beams are used in instrumental music to join consecutive eighth notes within a rhythmic unit. Beams do not extend across bar lines or connect unaccented notes to accented notes in conventional notation. Vocal music is beamed like instrumental music where two or more notes occur with a single word or syllable. Compare the following:

_____ It Came upon the Midnight Clear

The time signature for the example of vocal and instrumental notation is _____.
   6/8

A 6/8 time signature indicates that there are _____ beats in a measure and that the
          SIX

beats are represented by _____ notes.
           EIGHTH

The number of beats in a measure and the pattern of accents are the same in 6/8 and 6/4 time.

Only the note symbol used to represent the _____ is different. In both time signa-
           BEAT

tures the primary accent falls on the first beat of the measure. The secondary accent falls on the

_____ beat of the measure. The second, third, fifth, and sixth beats of the measure
     FOURTH

are _____.
        UNACCENTED

A note symbol not previously used appears in the 6/8 example. Can you name it?

♩.  _____  _____ note
        DOTTED              QUARTER

A *dotted quarter note* is equal to a quarter plus an eighth or to three _____ notes.

EIGHTH

$$\text{♩.} = \text{♩} + \text{♪} \quad \text{or} \quad \text{♪} + \text{♪} + \text{♪}$$

A dotted half note equals two dotted quarter notes.

$$\text{♩.}\!\!\!\!= \text{♩.} + \text{♩.}$$

The following rhythms are typical in measures of 6/8 time. Practice them until the proper responses to the notation are almost spontaneous. Vary the tempo (speed) from quite slow to moderately fast.

$$\frac{6}{8} \quad \text{♫♫ ♫♫} \mid \text{♩.} \quad \text{♩.} \mid \text{♩ ♪♪♩} \mid \text{♩.} \quad \| :$$

<u>1</u> 2 3 <u>4</u> 5 6   <u>1</u> 2 3 <u>4</u> 5 6   <u>1</u> 2 3 <u>4</u> 5 6   <u>1</u> 2 3 <u>4</u> 5 6

When an eighth note receives one beat:

a quarter note receives _____ beats,

TWO

a dotted quarter note receives _____ beats,

THREE

and a dotted half note receives _____ beats.

SIX

Write the single note which is rhythmically equivalent to each of the following groups of eighth notes.

$$\text{♫} = \underline{\quad\quad}$$
♩

$$\text{♫♪} = \underline{\quad\quad}$$
♩.

$$\text{♫♫} = \underline{\quad\quad}$$
♩.

In 6/8 time rhythmic values of four and five eighth notes are written with ties as shown. The second note of the tie comes on a secondary accent within the measure or on a primary accent across a bar line.

The relationship between an eighth note and an eighth rest is readily perceived.

Eighth note    ♪  =  𝄾    Eighth rest

Write the rest equivalent for all of the notes studied thus far.

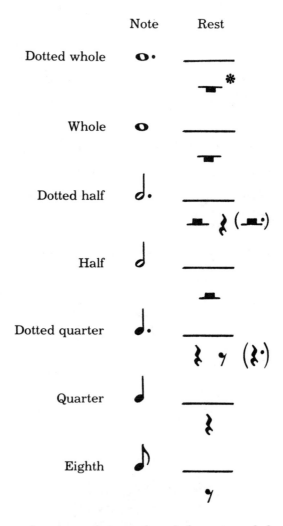

[*Note: It is not necessary to dot or supplement the whole rest symbol, since whole rests serve for complete measures of silence in all meters.]

Now you are ready to read the rhythm of this familiar song which has eighth notes and rests and dotted quarter notes in 6/8 time. It is a slow song, so establish an unhurried beat.

———— Drink to Me Only with Thine Eyes

When music in 6/8 time is fast, only the accents are heard and felt as beats. The eighth notes, which according to the time signature represent beats, are heard as divisions of the beat. The dotted-quarter value is perceived as the beat. There are two such beats in a measure, and each beat divides in thirds.

**Fast**

1 - - 2 - -     1 - - 2 - -     1 - - 2 - -     1 - - 2 - -

Syllables may be used in conjunction with the beat numbers as an aid in achieving rhythmically precise fractions of beats. The syllables generally associated with beats divided in thirds are *ONE, and, a, Two, and, a.* Pronounce the "a" like the indefinite article.

**Fast**

1 - - 2 - -     1 & a 2 & a     1 - a 2 & -     1 - - 2 - -

Establish a two-beat pattern by tapping or clapping and sing *Three Blind Mice*. The dotted quarter notes in the first measure should coincide with the beats. Eighth notes equal one third of a beat, and quarter notes equal two thirds of a beat.

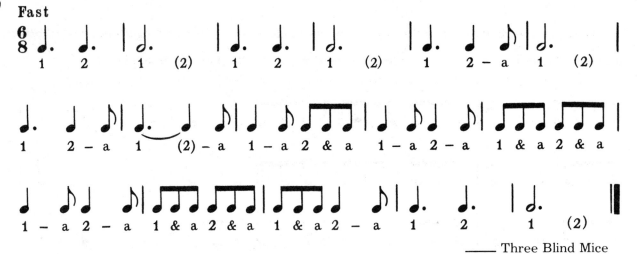

—— Three Blind Mice

While the rhythm of *Three Blind Mice* is fresh in your mind, tap a two-beat pattern and clap the rhythm of the melody without thinking of the words. Continue tapping the beat and sing the rhythm with the numbers and syllables written below the notes, omitting the numbers enclosed in parentheses. Learn to associate the numbers and syllables with the various rhythmic patterns, and utilize them in reading the rhythm of unfamiliar music.

It makes no difference in the relative values whether 6/8 time is regarded as having six eighth-note beats or two dotted-quarter-note beats in a measure. For the slower tempos counting in six is preferred. Counting in two is more practical for the faster tempos. The point at which the change takes place is a matter of personal preference.

Clap the rhythm of the following song while counting the beats aloud. Start with six moderately slow beats in a measure. Repeat the song several times, gradually increasing the speed. When it is no longer convenient to count six beats in a measure, switch to two. This sign ⌢ above a note means that the note should be held somewhat longer than its normal value. Ignore the sign while practicing the rhythm. Then perform the rhythm observing the sign to help you identify the song before looking at its name.

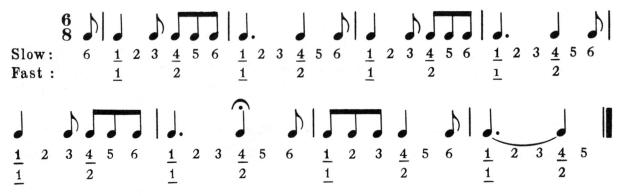

Name of song ——————————————

FOR HE'S A JOLLY GOOD FELLOW

This sign ⌢ is known as a *hold*, a *pause*, or a *fermata*. It signifies a momentary interruption of the rhythmic flow. When it is above a note or rest, the note or rest is prolonged beyond its normal value. The exact duration is left to the discretion of the performer or conductor. When the sign is above a bar line (between notes), the beat is suspended temporarily, and there is a moment of unmeasured silence, likewise at the discretion of the performer or conductor. The sign is also used to mark the end of a composition under certain circumstances. Return to *For He's a Jolly Good Fellow* and sing it with the words, observing the *hold* sign.

Two names are given for the sign below. Provide the third name, which is the shortest and easiest to remember.

⌢     Pause, fermata, or ————————————
                                             HOLD

✠     ✠     ✠     ✠

When the beat is represented by a quarter note, the beats divide in halves, and the half beats are represented by eighth notes. One quarter note equals ———————————— eighth notes. In
                                                   TWO
counting half beats write "&" and say "and." The counts are written under the notes of the 2/4 example as a model. Write the counts under the notes of the other two examples and practice all of the rhythms.

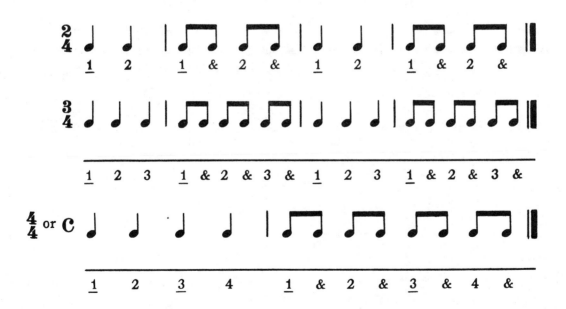

The following rhythms are from songs having eighth notes in 2/4, 3/4, 4/4, and common time. Write the counts under the notes if you find that helpful and read the rhythms according to the directions given for earlier exercises.

———Billy Boy

———While We Danced at the Mardi Gras

———Four in a Boat

———Red River Valley

Dotted quarter notes occur frequently in music which has quarter-note beats. When the beats are quarter notes, dotted quarter notes have a rhythmic value of one-and-a-half beats.

Perform the following rhythms which contain dotted quarter notes.

——In the Gloaming

——America

——Cockles and Mussels

——Deck the Halls

✠    ✠    ✠    ✠

Notes, except whole notes, have fractional names. In order of decreasing relative value they are: whole, half, _____, _____, and *sixteenth*. Sixteenth notes have
<br>QUARTER    EIGHTH
two flags or beams, and sixteenth rests have two hooks.

Sixteenth notes ♪ ♪ ♪ ♪ ♬♬♬

Sixteenth rest ♷

The sixteenth-note equivalents of all the note values previously studied, and also the dotted eighth note, are shown in the following example. Study this graphic representation of relative values and record the number of sixteenths in each note value.*

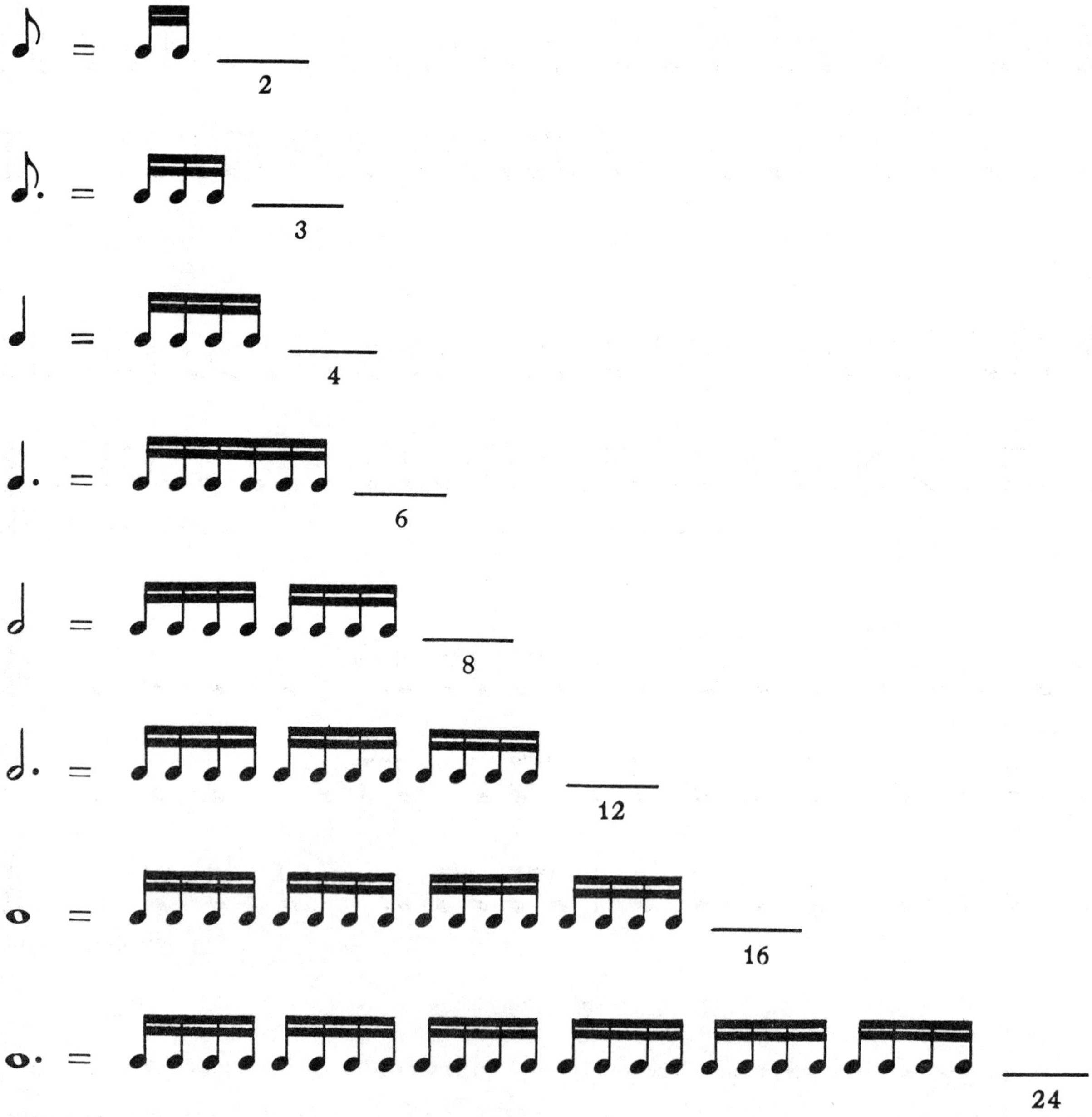

♪ = 𝅘𝅥𝅯𝅘𝅥𝅯 _____
2

♪. = 𝅘𝅥𝅯𝅘𝅥𝅯𝅘𝅥𝅯 _____
3

♩ = 𝅘𝅥𝅯𝅘𝅥𝅯𝅘𝅥𝅯𝅘𝅥𝅯 _____
4

♩. = 𝅘𝅥𝅯𝅘𝅥𝅯𝅘𝅥𝅯𝅘𝅥𝅯𝅘𝅥𝅯𝅘𝅥𝅯 _____
6

𝅗𝅥 = 𝅘𝅥𝅯𝅘𝅥𝅯𝅘𝅥𝅯𝅘𝅥𝅯 𝅘𝅥𝅯𝅘𝅥𝅯𝅘𝅥𝅯𝅘𝅥𝅯 _____
8

𝅗𝅥. = 𝅘𝅥𝅯𝅘𝅥𝅯𝅘𝅥𝅯𝅘𝅥𝅯 𝅘𝅥𝅯𝅘𝅥𝅯𝅘𝅥𝅯𝅘𝅥𝅯 𝅘𝅥𝅯𝅘𝅥𝅯𝅘𝅥𝅯𝅘𝅥𝅯 _____
12

𝅝 = 𝅘𝅥𝅯𝅘𝅥𝅯𝅘𝅥𝅯𝅘𝅥𝅯 𝅘𝅥𝅯𝅘𝅥𝅯𝅘𝅥𝅯𝅘𝅥𝅯 𝅘𝅥𝅯𝅘𝅥𝅯𝅘𝅥𝅯𝅘𝅥𝅯 𝅘𝅥𝅯𝅘𝅥𝅯𝅘𝅥𝅯𝅘𝅥𝅯 _____
16

𝅝. = 𝅘𝅥𝅯𝅘𝅥𝅯𝅘𝅥𝅯𝅘𝅥𝅯 𝅘𝅥𝅯𝅘𝅥𝅯𝅘𝅥𝅯𝅘𝅥𝅯 𝅘𝅥𝅯𝅘𝅥𝅯𝅘𝅥𝅯𝅘𝅥𝅯 𝅘𝅥𝅯𝅘𝅥𝅯𝅘𝅥𝅯𝅘𝅥𝅯 𝅘𝅥𝅯𝅘𝅥𝅯𝅘𝅥𝅯𝅘𝅥𝅯 𝅘𝅥𝅯𝅘𝅥𝅯𝅘𝅥𝅯𝅘𝅥𝅯 _____
24

[*Note: The beaming varies according to the time signature.]

Write single notes equal to the combined value of the sixteenths.

Complete the following equations, writing two notes with a combined value equal to each un-
dotted note and three notes with a combined value equal to each dotted note.

Repeat the next exercise several times in succession to gain facility in dividing beats in halves
and quarters. The method of tapping and counting shown may prove helpful in performing unfamiliar and complex rhythms. When counting fourths of beats, pronounce the first "a" as a long vowel
and the second like the indefinite article. The same rhythm is notated first in 2/4 and then in cut time.

The next two songs have sixteenth notes in 4/4 time and eighth notes in cut time, respectively. Practice their rhythms to develop skill in performing four notes in a beat.

Several rhythm patterns within quarter-note beats are produced by combining sixteenth notes in various ways. Transcribe the patterns in the manner of the model, substituting single notes for the tied sixteenths.

In the next example the notes are aligned to show the relationship of each pattern to a four-sixteenth or four-eighth division of a beat. Dashes fill in where notes are held longer than a fourth of a beat. Repeat each pattern until the correct response to the notation is automatic. Then practice the various patterns in succession and in random order. Maintain a steady beat, slightly stressing the beginning of each group. This stress is particularly important in patterns with the shorter value on the beat.

The following rhythms include the more usual divided beat patterns. Perform each example before looking at the name of the song from which it is taken.

——Clementine

——I've Been Workin' on the Railroad

——Dixie

——The Blue Tail Fly

——Hush, Little Baby

——The Japanese Sandman

38

Sixteenth notes in 6/8 time provide opportunities for several new rhythm patterns. The two most common ones are shown in consecutive measures and then in a familiar context. Practice the abstract patterns and then the song rhythm which utilizes them.

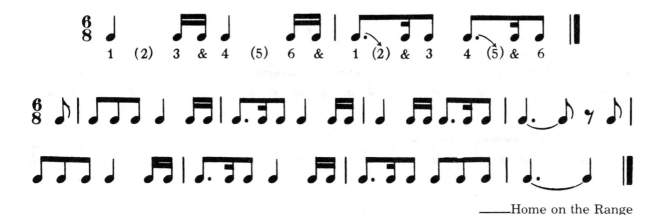

1  (2)  3  &  4  (5)  6  &  1  (2)  &  3  4  (5)  &  6

——Home on the Range

These rhythms occur in fast 6/8 time with two beats to the —————————— as well as in

MEASURE

slow 6/8 time with —————————— beats to the measure.

SIX

Division into thirds of values which normally divide in halves is indicated by a "3" above or below three notes comprising a group. Such groups are *triplets*. Three equal notes within an eighth, quarter, half, or whole value are ——————————.

TRIPLETS

Beat

Triplets

Perform the following rhythm while tapping a two-beat pattern. The exercise in 2/4 time with the triplets should duplicate exactly the 6/8 rhythm.

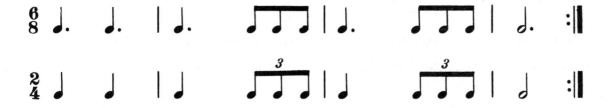

Practice these rhythms, dividing the beats precisely in thirds where triplets are indicated.

——Row, Row, Row Your Boat

——Sing We Together

Division into halves of values which normally divide in thirds is indicated by a "2" above or below two notes. Such pairs of notes are *duplets*. Two equal notes with a combined value of a dotted note are ————————————————.

DUPLETS

Dotted note

Duplets

Establish a two-beat pattern and perform these rhythms. The duplets in 6/8 time should sound like the eighths in 2/4.

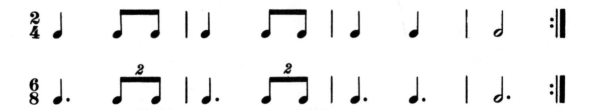

*La Paloma (The Dove)* is written in 2/4 time with many triplets, but it could be written in 6/8 time with duplets, as shown. To be identical in sound, the 6/8 version would require duplets in the incomplete measures.

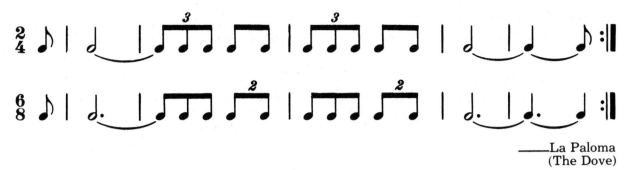

—La Paloma
(The Dove)

In complicated music, numbers other than 2 and 3, like 5, 6, 7, etc., are used occasionally to indicate division of a rhythmic unit into the specified number of equal parts.

When a weak beat is tied to a stronger beat or the end of one beat is tied to the beginning of the next causing a temporary displacement of the normal rhythmic division, the effect is known as *syncopation*. Stated another way, when a note introduced in an unstressed portion of a beat or measure extends into the following beat or measure anticipating or delaying the expected rhythmic event, the effect is known as _____. Arrows point to syncopations in the following example.

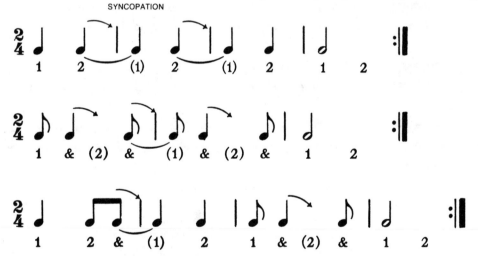

Accompany these syncopated rhythms with prominent background beats, which must remain perfectly regular against the shifting accents of the syncopation.

—Buffalo Gals

42

——Joshua Fit the Battle of Jericho

——Michael, Row the Boat Ashore

The next several song rhythms illustrate some of the less usual time signatures. Perform each one and be prepared to answer questions about it.

——Bring a Torch, Jeannette, Isabella

With reference to the previous song, *Bring a Torch, Jeannette, Isabella:*

What is the time signature?_____
3/8

How many beats are there in a measure?_____
THREE

What kind of note represents the beat?_____
EIGHTH

Which beat of the measure receives a primary accent?_____
FIRST

Are there any secondary accents?_____
NO

——Beautiful Dreamer

What is the time signature of *Beautiful Dreamer?*———————————

In 9/8 time, as in 6/8, the eighth or the dotted quarter value may be perceived as the beat. When

the tempo is slow, the perceived beat is apt to be represented by an———————— note.

EIGHTH

When the tempo is fast, the perceived beat is more apt to be a dotted———————— value.

QUARTER

*Beautiful Dreamer* is a borderline case. Write the counts under the notes of its rhythm, first for

eighth-note beats and then for dotted-quarter-note beats.

♪ Beat

♩. Beat

| ♪ Beat | 1 2 3 4 5 6 7 8 9 | 1 2 3 4 5 6 7 8 9 | 1 2 3 4 5 6 7 8 9 | 1 2 3 4 5 6 7 8 9 |
|--------|-------------------|-------------------|-------------------|-------------------|
| ♩. Beat | 1 & a 2     3 | 1 & a 2    (3) | 1 & a 2 & a 3 & a | 1    (2)    (3) |

——Soldiers' Chorus

The *Soldiers' Chorus* is in ———————— time. Twelve-eight time can have twelve

12/8

eighth-note beats or four dotted-quarter-note beats in a measure. The dotted quarter value invari-

ably is taken as the beat in performing the *Soldiers' Chorus*. The four beats of 12/8 measures receive

a *primary accent*, a *secondary accent*, or *no accent* as follows:

First Beat, ———————— ————————

PRIMARY ACCENT

Second beat, ———————— ————————

NO ACCENT

Third beat, ———————— ————————

SECONDARY ACCENT

Fourth beat, ———————— ————————

NO ACCENT

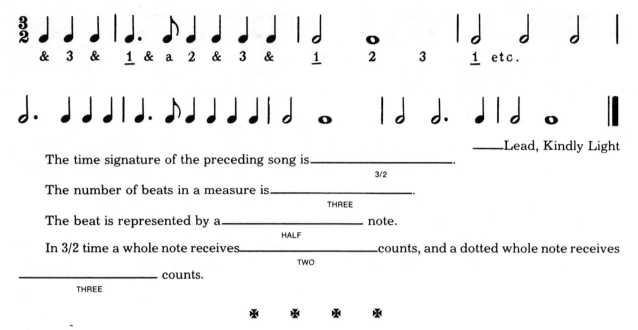

——Lead, Kindly Light

The time signature of the preceding song is_____.
                                                3/2
The number of beats in a measure is_____.
                                           THREE
The beat is represented by a_____ note.
                                    HALF
In 3/2 time a whole note receives_____counts, and a dotted whole note receives
                                      TWO
_____ counts.
  THREE

✠    ✠    ✠    ✠

You now have learned and practiced all of the usual time signatures. Demonstrate that you understand them by writing one measure showing the beat pattern for each time signature indicated. Number the beats and underline the numbers of accented beats, both primary and secondary.

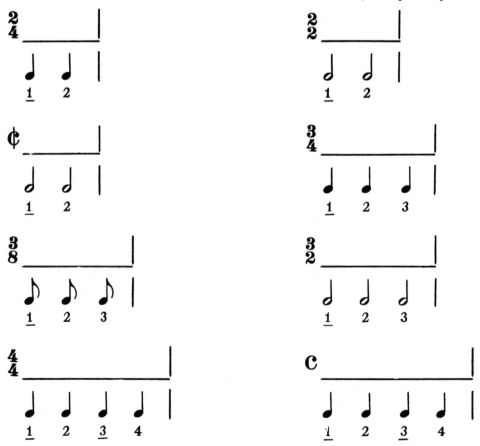

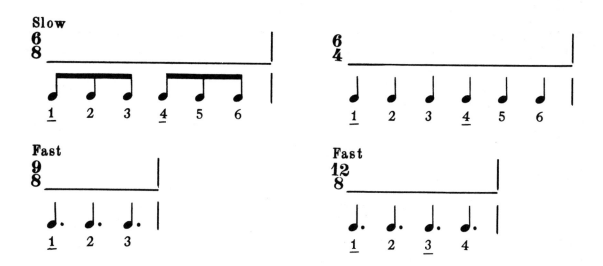

The symbols which represent the beats and their normal divisions are shown in the following tables.

| Time Signatures | Beats | Divisions |
|---|---|---|
| $\frac{2}{2}$ ¢ $\frac{3}{2}$ | 𝅗𝅥 | 𝅘𝅥 𝅘𝅥 𝅘𝅥𝅮𝅘𝅥𝅮𝅘𝅥𝅮𝅘𝅥𝅮  1 & 2 a & a |
| $\frac{2}{4}$ $\frac{3}{4}$ $\frac{4}{4}$ C $\frac{6}{4}$ | 𝅘𝅥 | 𝅘𝅥𝅮𝅘𝅥𝅮 𝅘𝅥𝅯𝅘𝅥𝅯𝅘𝅥𝅯𝅘𝅥𝅯  1 & 2 a & a |
| $\frac{3}{8}$ $\frac{6}{8}$ $\frac{9}{8}$ $\frac{12}{8}$ | 𝅘𝅥𝅮 | 𝅘𝅥𝅯𝅘𝅥𝅯 𝅘𝅥𝅰𝅘𝅥𝅰𝅘𝅥𝅰𝅘𝅥𝅰 *  1 & 2 a & a |

[*Note: Thirty-second notes. Explained on page 48.]

There is no time signature which specifies a dotted note as the beat, but dotted values may be perceived as beats in faster tempos. These additional interpretations of the time signatures result:

| Time Signatures | Beats | Divisions |
|---|---|---|
| $\frac{3}{8}$ $\frac{6}{8}$ $\frac{9}{8}$ $\frac{12}{8}$ | 𝅘𝅥. | 𝅘𝅥𝅮𝅘𝅥𝅮𝅘𝅥𝅮 𝅘𝅥𝅯𝅘𝅥𝅯𝅘𝅥𝅯𝅘𝅥𝅯𝅘𝅥𝅯𝅘𝅥𝅯 |
| $\frac{3}{4}$ $\frac{6}{4}$ | 𝅗𝅥. | 𝅘𝅥𝅘𝅥𝅘𝅥 𝅘𝅥𝅮𝅘𝅥𝅮𝅘𝅥𝅮𝅘𝅥𝅮𝅘𝅥𝅮𝅘𝅥𝅮 |

Compare and contrast the beat patterns and divisions in the following measures.

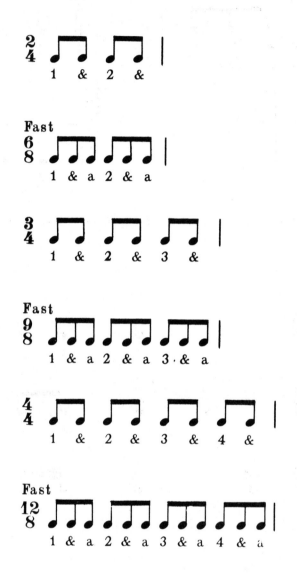

Which time signatures have:

Two beats in a measure?_____ _____
                                   2/4                          6/8

Six eighth notes in a measure?_____ _____
                                        6/8                       3/4

Two three-note groups in a measure?_____
                                              6/8

Three two-note groups in a measure?_____
                                              3/4

Four three-note groups in a measure?_____
                                              12/8

Make all of the following notes eighths by adding beams to groups of two or three appropriate to the time signature.

Clap and count the beat patterns of all the time signatures illustrated on pages 44–46. Then count the beats and clap appropriate divisions. Repeat each one several times in succession before proceeding to the next. Observe that some patterns can be notated and some time signatures can be interpreted in more than one way.

When all of the patterns are thoroughly familiar, try to detect them in the music you hear. You should have no difficulty in distinguishing between the basic two-beat and three-beat patterns. It is more difficult, and not always possible, to recognize the combinations of these patterns. You cannot tell which note symbol represents the beat, because this is not reflected in the sound.

Time signatures other than those listed are possible but uncommon in familiar music and that composed prior to this century. The intricate rhythms of contemporary music often involve frequent changes of meter and unusual time signatures. Such complexities are perhaps beyond your performing ability but not beyond your comprehension. All rhythmic notation is governed by principles you have already encountered. In the remaining pages of Part I these principles are summarized and their application is extended to logical limits.

Quarter, eighth, and half notes (sometimes with dots) are used to notate beats without particular regard for absolute duration. Beats which are fast, slow, and in between may be represented by any one of the note symbols. In different contexts the various note symbols may represent identical durations and the same symbol, different durations. That is to say, the duration of any note symbol varies from composition to composition, but within a given context the fractional names of notes reflect precise rhythmic relationships. A half note is always half as long as a _____ note.
WHOLE
A half note is always twice as long as a _____ note.
QUARTER

Each flag or beam halves the value of a note. Complete the table.

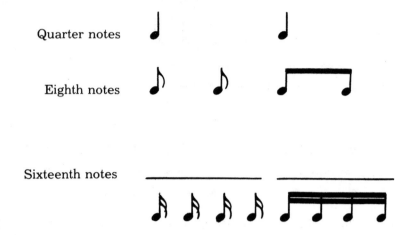

Quarter notes

Eighth notes

Sixteenth notes

Continuing the process produces *thirty-second notes* and *sixty-fourth notes*. They are shown with corresponding rests.

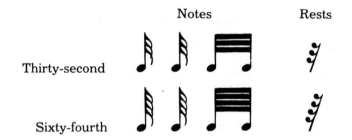

Such small fractional values are generally avoided for obvious reasons.

*Double whole notes* exist but are not often found outside of historical editions of old music. As the name implies, one double whole note equals two _____ notes.

WHOLE

Double whole note

Double whole rest

The next two tables name an equivalent for every note value. Complete the tables by inserting the missing note symbols. Where flags or beams are required, flag single notes and beam groups.

|  | ONE | ←EQUALS→ | TWO |  |
|---|---|---|---|---|
| Double whole note | 𝆹𝅝 | = | 𝅝  𝅝 | Whole notes |
| Whole note |  | = |  | Half notes |
| Half note |  | = |  | Quarter notes |
| Quarter note |  | = |  | Eighth notes |
| Eighth note |  | = |  | Sixteenth notes |
| Sixteenth note |  | = |  | Thirty-second notes |
| Thirty-second note |  | = |  | Sixty-fourth notes |

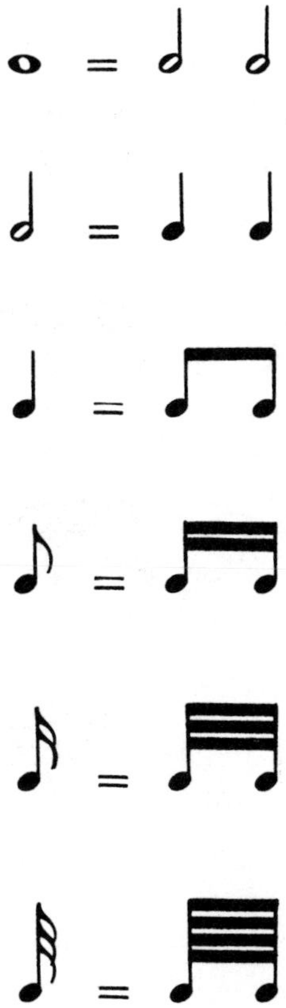

𝅝 = 𝅗𝅥 𝅗𝅥

𝅗𝅥 = 𝅘𝅥 𝅘𝅥

𝅘𝅥 = 𝅘𝅥𝅮𝅘𝅥𝅮

𝅘𝅥𝅮 = 𝅘𝅥𝅯𝅘𝅥𝅯

𝅘𝅥𝅯 = 𝅘𝅥𝅰𝅘𝅥𝅰

𝅘𝅥𝅰 = 𝅘𝅥𝅱𝅘𝅥𝅱

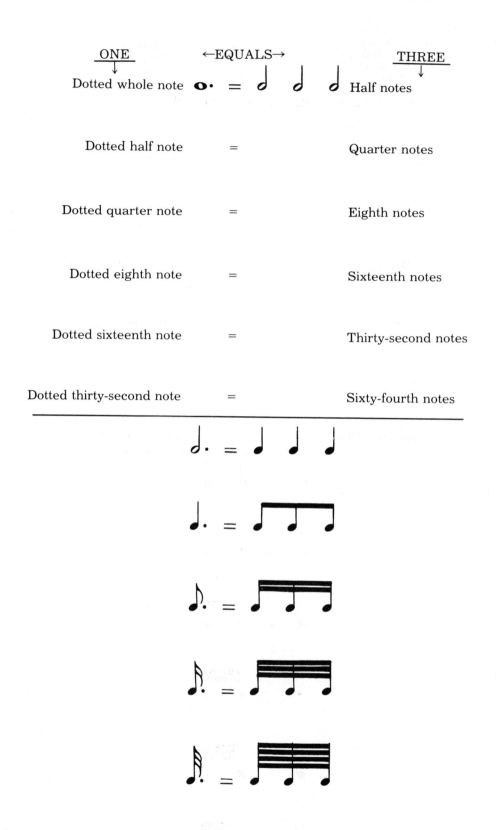

|  | ONE | ←EQUALS→ |  | THREE |  |
|---|---|---|---|---|---|
| Dotted whole note | 𝅝· | = | ♩ ♩ ♩ | | Half notes |
| Dotted half note | | = | | | Quarter notes |
| Dotted quarter note | | = | | | Eighth notes |
| Dotted eighth note | | = | | | Sixteenth notes |
| Dotted sixteenth note | | = | | | Thirty-second notes |
| Dotted thirty-second note | | = | | | Sixty-fourth notes |

Eighth notes serve as a common denominator in representing graphically the relative values of the other notes in the following diagram.

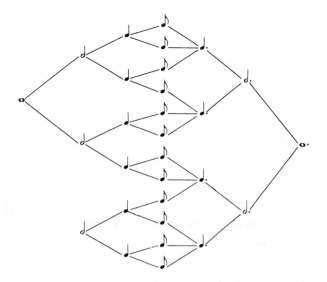

Here is another way of representing graphically the relative values of the various notes. Dotted notes or equivalent groupings appear on alternate lines.

This concludes the study of rhythmic notation. Now you are ready to proceed to the study of pitch notation.

# pitch

*High* and *low* are terms which describe pitch. Changes in pitch are either *up* or *down*. Pitch can be represented by the position of notes on a page.

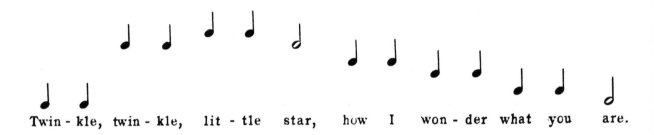

Continue notating the pitches in a similar way above the words of the second line of the song.

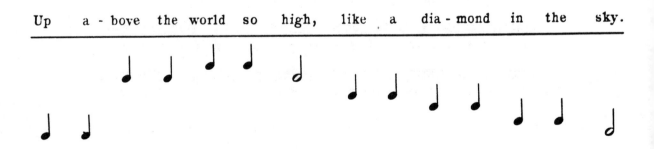

To represent pitch with precision, notes are placed on a *staff* consisting of five equally spaced lines.

Staff

The five lines of a _____ are numbered consecutively from bottom to top.
STAFF

Staff lines 5 4 3 2 1

The five lines of a staff enclose four *spaces*. The four _____ are numbered
SPACES
similarly from bottom to top.

Staff spaces 4 3 2 1

Each line and each space represents a different pitch. The number of different pitches which can be written on the five lines and in the four spaces of a staff is _____. An extra pitch
NINE
can be written below the first line and another one above the fifth line for a total of _____.
ELEVEN
The eleven pitches are shown in order from low to high.

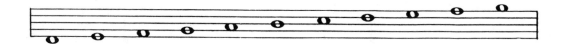

Write the same eleven pitches in descending order from high to low. Notes in spaces touch the lines on both sides of the space. Notes of the same size are centered on the lines.

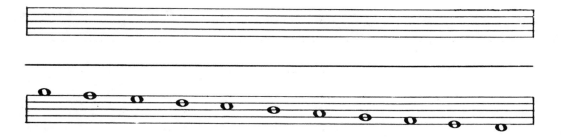

54

Notes with stems may be turned either way, with the stems going up or down from the note head. The direction of the stem has no effect on the meaning of the note.

When a note is turned upside down, the stem changes from one side of the head to the other. Stems going up are on the right side of the head. Stems going down are on the ———————— LEFT side of the head. Add stems alternating up and down to make quarter notes.

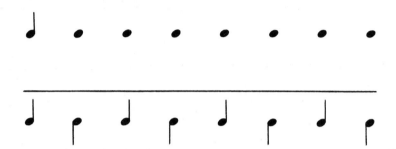

The direction of the stem is determined by the location of the note on the staff. The stems on notes below the middle (third) line go up. Add stems in the proper direction to note heads which do not have them.

The stems of notes above the middle (third) line go down. Add stems in the proper direction to note heads which do not have them.

The stems of notes on the middle line may go either up or down, as shown. Add stems to the other note heads to make quarter and half notes.

Flags always go on the right side of the stem. Copy the eighth and sixteenth notes in the blank measure, duplicating the direction of the stems and flags.

Beams joining groups of notes follow the general contour of the group. The stems of a beamed group all go in the same direction. When the group crosses the middle line, the stems go in the direction dictated by the majority of the notes or in the direction that places the beam nearer the center of the staff. Following these principles, add stems and beams to convert the note heads into groups of four sixteenth notes.

To notate pitches above and below the staff, *ledger lines* are used. Ledger LINES just long enough to be visible on both sides of a note head are spaced like staff lines above and below the staff. Ledger lines serve to extend the staff in both directions. Notes are written on, above, and below _____ lines as shown.

LEDGER

The pitch relationship between two notes is shown by their relative location. Higher pitches are higher on the staff. Lower pitches are _____ on the staff. Indicate whether the

LOWER

second note of the following pairs is *higher* or *lower* than the first.

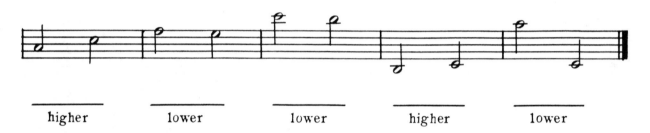

| higher | lower | lower | higher | lower |

Pitch relationships are shown by location on the staff. Each line and space of the staff is given a specific pitch meaning by a *clef sign*. A _____ sign appears at the beginning of

CLEF

each staff. The clef sign on the following staff is a *treble clef* sign.

Treble clef sign

Draw a treble clef sign on each section of the staff. The size and general outline should approximate that of the printed symbol, but it is not necessary to duplicate the details.

Typical manuscript symbols

When a treble clef sign appears on the staff, the music is written *in the treble clef*. The following notation of *Twinkle, Twinkle, Little Star* is in the treble clef. Sing the melody and observe the relationship between the sound of the pitches and their location on the staff. The rhythmic notation is already familiar.

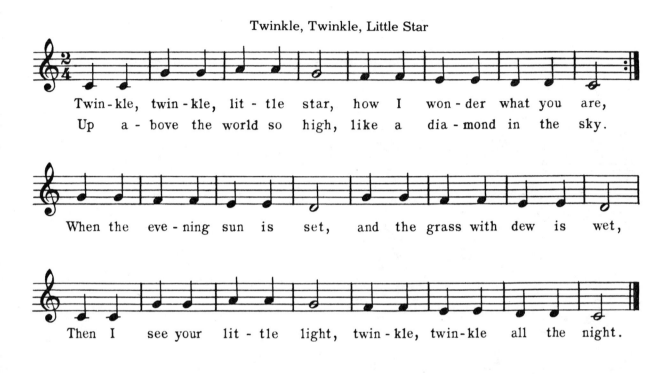

Twinkle, Twinkle, Little Star

The time signature is given only once, at the beginning of the song, but a clef sign appears on every line. The first symbol on the staff is a _____ sign. The clef sign gives specific
CLEF
pitch meaning to the lines and spaces of the staff. The clef sign used in the notation of *Twinkle, Twinkle, Little Star* is a _____ clef.
TREBLE
Notes and pitches are identified by *letter names*. In the treble _____ the note
CLEF
in the second space is A.

A

The first seven letters of the alphabet are used to name the notes in ascending order. Fill in the missing letter names.

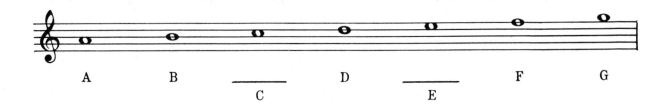

A      B      ___      D      ___      F      G
                    C                    E

The letters of the alphabet are reversed when the notes are in descending order. Fill in the missing letter names.

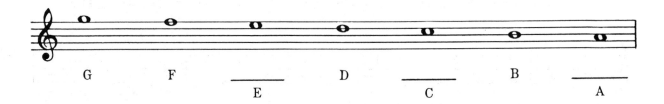

G      F      ___      D      ___      B      ___
                    E                    C                    A

The letter names of the following notes spell words. Write the letter names below the notes. If in doubt about a note name, start from second-space A and say the letter names of the lines and spaces up to the note in question.

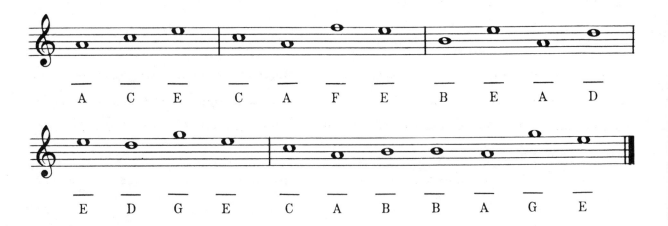

A    C    E     C    A    F    E     B    E    A    D

E    D    G    E     C    A    B    B    A    G    E

The seven letters, A through G, are repeated in cycles as note names. After G, the series begins again with A. Thus the letter names of the next 14 notes above A in ascending order are:

A  B  C  D  E  F  G  A  _____
                                  B  C  D  E  F  G  A

The order of the letter names is reversed for the notes in descending order. Complete the series of letter names in descending order.

A  G  F  E  D  C  B  A  _____
                        G   F   E   D   C   B   A

The order of the letter names, both ascending and descending, is apparent when they are arranged in a circle.

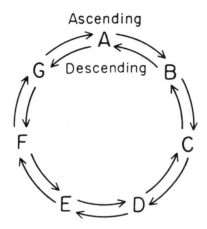

Ascending:

    The next letter name after B is _____.
                                                    C

    The next letter name after D is _____.
                                                    E

    The next letter name after F is _____.
                                                    G

    The next letter name after G is _____.
                                                    A

Descending:

    The next letter name after A is _____.
                                                    G

    The next letter name after F is _____.
                                                    E

    The next letter name after D is _____.
                                                    C

    The next letter name after B is _____.
                                                    A

The difference in pitch between two notes is an *interval*. The _____ between
                                                                  INTERVAL
two notes with the same letter name is an *octave*. *Octave* comes from a word meaning *eight*. When the letter names are written in order, the eighth is the same as the first. The letter names from A to A are written above the numbers. Write the letter names from C to C below the numbers.

The interval from A to A is an octave. The interval from C to C is an ———————————. The
                                                                    OCTAVE
six different notes between any two notes with the same letter name are *in an octave.*

The octaves are bracketed in the next example, and some of the letter names are given. Supply
the missing letter names.

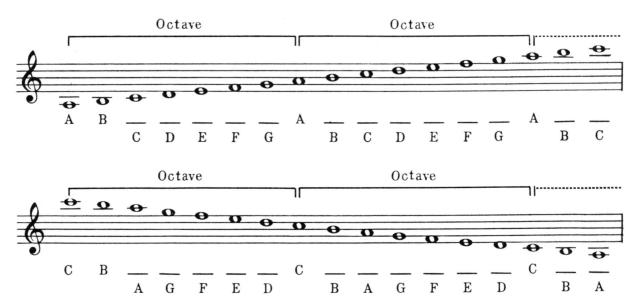

The interval between the lowest note and the highest note in the preceding example is two notes
more than two octaves. Each letter name is used once in the first octave and is repeated in the
second octave. Some are used a third time in the incomplete third octave. Notes with the same
letter name are very similar in sound.

From low to high, the letter names of the four spaces in the treble clef are F, A, C, and E. The
letter names of the four spaces spell the word ———————————. Write the letter names below
                                                FACE
the notes.

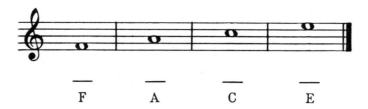

From low to high, the letter names of the five lines in the treble clef are E, G, B, D, and F. The letter names of the five lines can be associated with the initial letters of the words *Every Good Boy Deserves Friends*. Write the letter names under the notes.

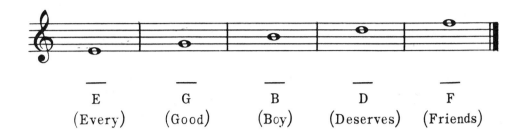

| E | G | B | D | F |
|---|---|---|---|---|
| (Every) | (Good) | (Boy) | (Deserves) | (Friends) |

Memorize the letter names of the lines and spaces as an aid to quick recognition of notes in the treble clef. Now name these notes.

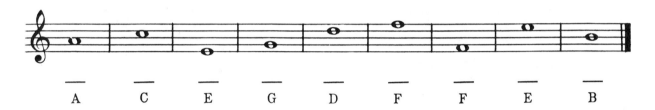

A    C    E    G    D    F    F    E    B

Write the missing letter names under the notes of *Twinkle, Twinkle, Little Star*.

Twinkle, Twinkle, Little Star

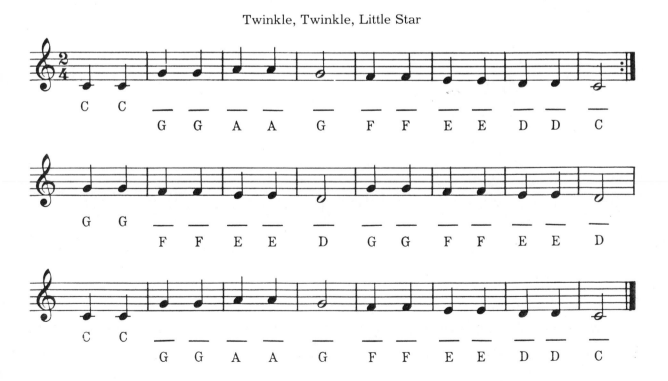

C  C  G  G  A  A  G  F  F  E  E  D  D  C

G  G  F  F  E  E  D  G  G  F  F  E  E  D

C  C  G  G  A  A  G  F  F  E  E  D  D  C

The letter name of any note can be determined by starting from a known note and saying the letter names of the intervening lines and spaces in order. To determine the letter name of the note on the second ledger line below the staff, for example, start from the first-line E (as in Every) and go backward through the alphabet to A. Write the letter names below the solid note heads.

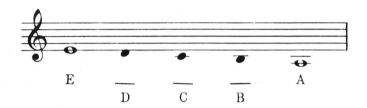

    E     ——    ——    ——    A

          D      C     B

To determine the letter name of the note on the second ledger line above the staff, start from the fifth-line F (as in Friends) and go through the letter names to C. Remember, A follows G. Write the letter names below the solid note heads.

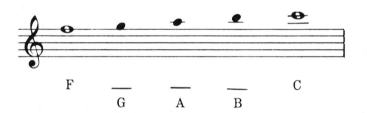

    F     ——    ——    ——    C

          G      A     B

Name these notes written in the treble clef.

   D     G     B     B     A     A     A     C     C     C

Write the specified notes in the treble clef in at least two octaves, and in three if possible, using no more than two ledger lines above or below the staff.

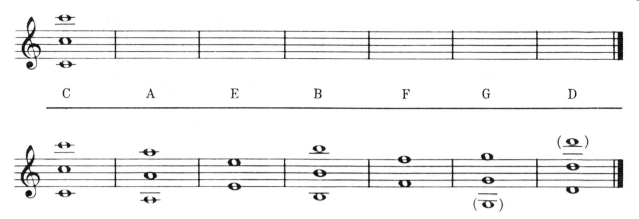

The low G and the high D in parentheses, not introduced previously, can be written with two ledger lines as shown.

✠　✠　✠　✠

Notes become tones when they are sung or played. The most convenient and generally available means for producing tones are the voice and the piano. Everyone is experienced in making sounds with the voice. The piano is an instrument upon which beginners can produce pitches accurately, and its keyboard makes pitch relationships visible. Both of these mediums are invaluable in learning to read music. Music reading skills developed with reference to the voice and the piano transfer readily to other instruments.

The full piano keyboard is shown with the letter names on the keys. The section of the keyboard used to play the notes from A below the treble staff to C above the treble staff is bracketed.

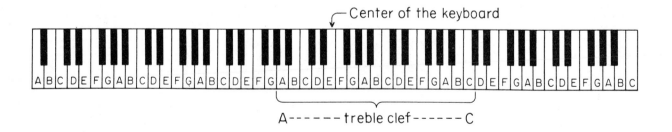

The bracketed section of the keyboard is enlarged in the next illustration. Notes of the treble clef are aligned with the keys upon which they are played. In this and subsequent illustrations only a section of the keyboard is shown.

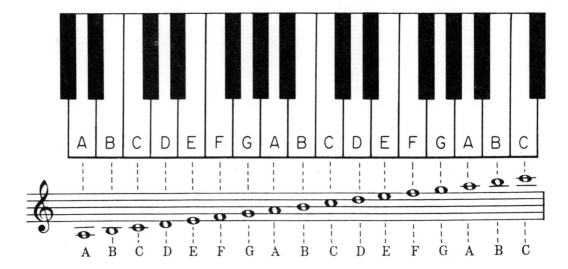

[*When the suggestion is made in the following pages to play an example on the piano, the notes may be located instead on the tear-out keyboard (pages 70–71). To gain greater familiarity with the piano, actually play all of the examples, even when the directions are to locate or sing the notes. If your interest is limited to the visual comprehension of musical notation, the performance suggestions may be disregarded.*]

Play the notes shown in the preceding example from left to right in succession. Say the letter     c
name as you strike each key. Then play the notes and say the letter names in reverse order, from right to left. Going from left to right the pitches become higher. Going from right to left the pitches become _____. Treble clef notes, as a rule, are played on the right
               LOWER
hand.

All of the notes introduced thus far are played on the white keys of the piano. Each note occupies a unique position in relation to the alternating groups of two and three black keys. The note between each group of two black keys is D. The letter name is printed on one D in the keyboard diagram. Write the letter name on the other D.

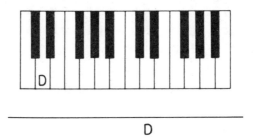

D

The note on the right of each group of two black keys is E. The note above D is _____.
                                                                                    E
The letter name is printed on one E in the keyboard diagram. Write the letter name on the other E.

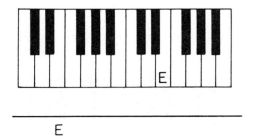

E

The note on the left of each group of two black keys is C. The note below D is ——————.
C

Write the letter names on both C's in the keyboard diagram.

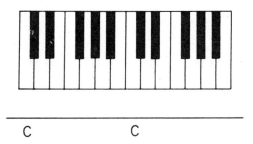

C          C

Write the letter names on the keys which have arrows pointing to them.

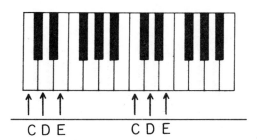

C D E      C D E

The note on the left of the groups of three black keys is F. The note above E is ——————.
F

Write the letter name on the F's.

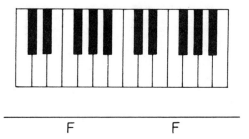

F          F

The note on the right of the groups of three black keys is B. The note below C is _____.

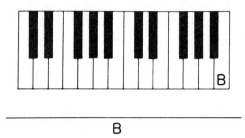

The letter name is printed on one B. Write the letter name on the other B.

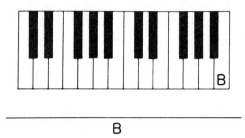

B

Write the letter names on the keys above the arrows.

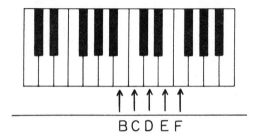

B C D E F

The two white keys within the group of three black keys are G and A. G is on the left. A is on the

_____. The note above G is _____. The note below A is _____.

RIGHT               A                 G

Write the letter names on the G and A keys.

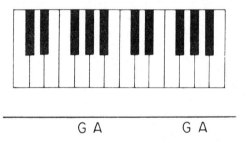

G A          G A

Write the letter names on the white keys between the two A's.

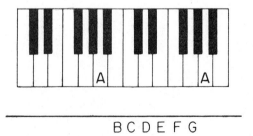

B C D E F G

Play the notes from A to A both ascending and descending. Say the letter name as you strike each key.

Write the letter names on the white keys between the C and A.

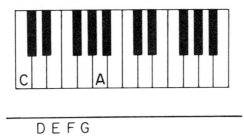

D E F G

Play the notes from C to A both ascending and descending. Start with the C just below (to the left of) the middle of the keyboard. Sing the pitches with letter names as you play them.

The notes from C to A are used in *Long, Long Ago*. In preparation for playing the part of the melody notated below, clap the rhythm slowly. Next, place the right thumb on the C nearest the middle of the keyboard. The fingers will fall naturally over or near the other keys used in playing the melody. Strike each key lightly with the finger which is most convenient and hold the key down for the duration of the note. Release the key as the next note is played. Since the melody is well known, you can tell by the sound if you make a mistake. The tempo may be slow, but the beat should be steady.

Long, Long Ago

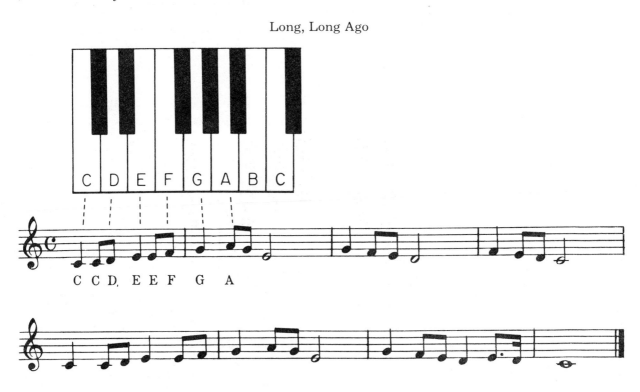

Sing *Long, Long Ago* using the letter names in place of the words.

In playing the piano, plan ahead and when possible place the fingers in advance over the keys they are to play. Since the objective of this book is to teach music reading, no attempt is made to teach piano fingerings.

*Twinkle, Twinkle, Little Star* contains the same notes as *Long, Long Ago.* Sing it with letter names and play it on the piano. In playing the melody, start with the thumb on the C key.

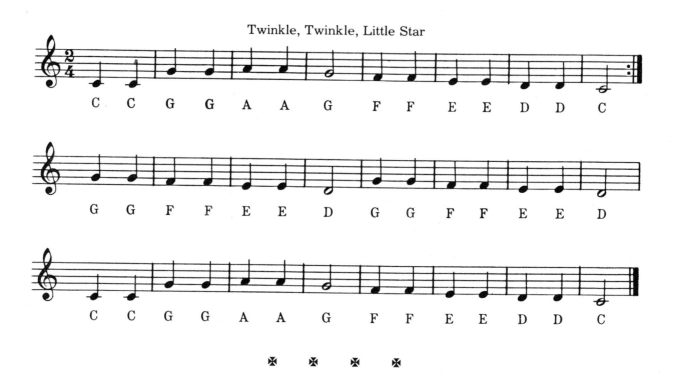

Twinkle, Twinkle, Little Star

C   C   G   G   A   A   G   F   F   E   E   D   D   C

G   G   F   F   E   E   D   G   G   F   F   E   E   D

C   C   G   G   A   A   G   F   F   E   E   D   D   C

Play the notes from C to C in succession and sing the pitches with letter names.

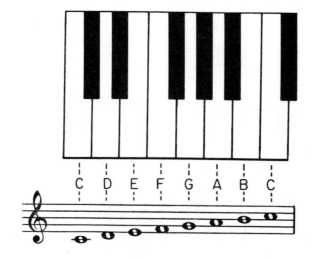

C  D  E  F  G  A  B  C

Tear out this page and keep the diagram of the keyboard on the opposite side available for ready reference while studying Part Two, Pitch.

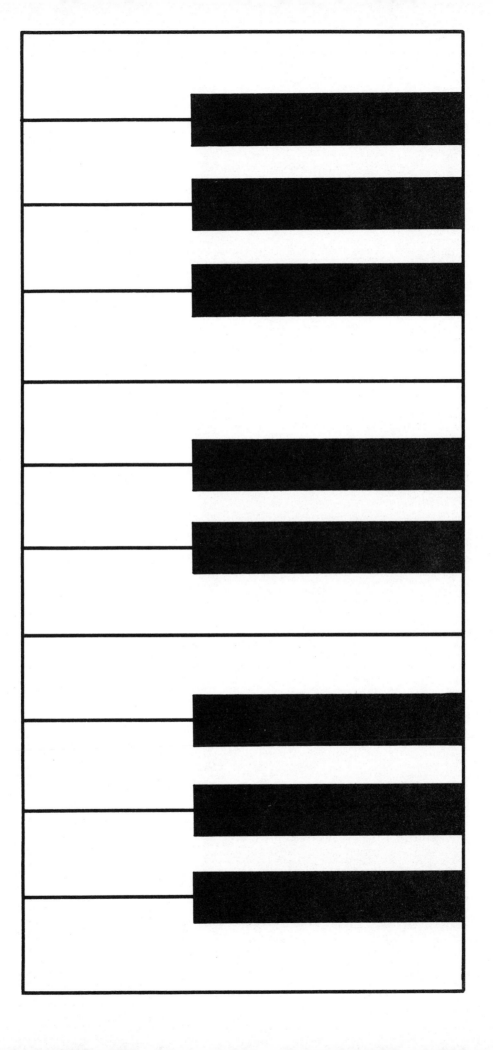

CUT OUT PAGE ON DOTTED LINE

Tear out this page and attach it to the preceding page, matching the two diagrams to make a continuous keyboard.

This note pattern should sound familiar. It is a *major scale*. Scales are identified by the letter name of the note upon which they begin and end. This scale begins and ends on C. It is a _____ major scale.
C

Melodies which derive their notes from a C major scale are *in the key* of C major. *Long, Long Ago* and *Twinkle, Twinkle, Little Star* are in the _____ of C major.
KEY

The note upon which a scale begins and ends is the *keynote*. The _____ of C major is C. Scales and keys are identified by the letter name of the keynote. When the keynote of a major scale is C, the scale is a _____ major scale. A melody which derives its notes from a C major scale is in the key of C _____.
KEYNOTE                                         C                                                    MAJOR

Melodies often begin and nearly always end on the keynote. The keynote of C major is _____. *Long, Long Ago* and *Twinkle, Twinkle, Little Star* are in the key of C _____. Both songs end on the keynote. The keynote is _____.
C                                         MAJOR                                         C

The notes of a scale are numbered consecutively from the keynote up to the keynote an octave higher. The first keynote is numbered 1. The keynote an octave higher is numbered 8 and/or 1 again. Write the missing numbers under the notes of the C major scale.

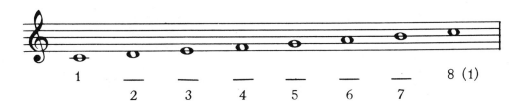

1 ___ ___ ___ ___ ___ ___ 8 (1)
   2   3   4   5   6   7

Each note of a scale is a *scale degree*. A scale degree is identified by the number corresponding to its position in the scale.

The first degree of a C major scale is _____.
C

The second degree of a C major scale is _____.
D

The third degree of a C major scale is _____.
E

The fourth degree of a C major scale is _____.
F

The fifth degree of a C major scale is _____.
G

The sixth degree of a C major scale is _____.
A

The seventh degree of a C major scale is _____.
B

The eighth degree of a C major scale is _____.
C

Each scale degree has a syllable name which is associated with its position in the scale. The syllable name of the keynote is *do*. In ascending order the syllable names are: *do, re, mi, fa, sol, la, ti,* and *do* (the keynote an octave higher). Sing the C major scale with number names and syllable names.

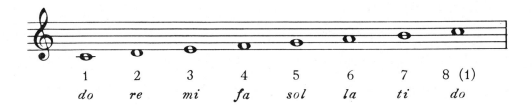

|  | 1 | 2 | 3 | 4 | 5 | 6 | 7 | 8 (1) |
|---|---|---|---|---|---|---|---|---|
|  | *do* | *re* | *mi* | *fa* | *sol* | *la* | *ti* | *do* |

The letter names and scale degrees of a descending C major scale are given. Write the syllable names in the third column.

C Major Scale

| Letter Name | Scale Degree | Syllable Name |
|---|---|---|
| C | 8(1) | *do* |
| B | 7 | *ti* |
| A | 6 | *la* |
| G | 5 | *sol* |
| F | 4 | *fa* |
| E | 3 | *mi* |
| D | 2 | *re* |
| C | 1 | *do* |

The difference in pitch between two notes is an *interval*. From C to D is an _____.
INTERVAL
From D to E is an _____. The difference in pitch between any two notes is an
INTERVAL
_____.
INTERVAL

The intervals between consecutive notes of a major scale are *whole steps* and *half steps*. The interval is a *whole step* when there is a black key between the two white keys. There is a black key between C and D. The interval between C and D is a whole _____. There is a
STEP
black key between D and E. The interval between D and E is a _____ step.
WHOLE

The interval between two white keys which have no black key between them is a *half step*.

There is no black key between E and F. The interval between E and F is a half _____.
STEP

There is no black key between B and C. The interval between B and C is a _____
HALF

step. The half steps and whole steps are marked on the following keyboard diagram.

Half steps

Whole steps

A major scale has a distinctive pattern of whole steps and half steps.

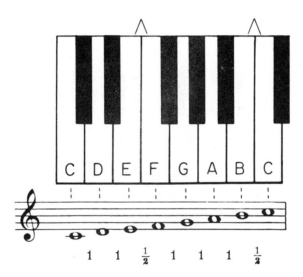

$$1 \quad 1 \quad \tfrac{1}{2} \quad 1 \quad 1 \quad 1 \quad \tfrac{1}{2}$$

Mark the whole steps (1) and the half steps ($\tfrac{1}{2}$) between the number names of a C major scale.

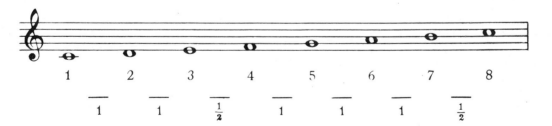

1   2   3   4   5   6   7   8

$$1 \quad\quad 1 \quad\quad \tfrac{1}{2} \quad\quad 1 \quad\quad 1 \quad\quad 1 \quad\quad \tfrac{1}{2}$$

In major scales the half steps are between 3 and 4 and between _____ and
7

_____.
8

Mark the whole steps (1) and the half steps ($\tfrac{1}{2}$) between the syllable names of a C major scale.

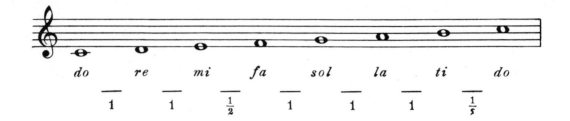

|     |     |     |     |     |     |     |
| --- | --- | --- | --- | --- | --- | --- |
| do  | re  | mi  | fa  | sol | la  | ti  | do |
| 1   | 1   | $\frac{1}{2}$ | 1   | 1   | 1   | $\frac{1}{2}$ |

In major scales the half steps are between *mi* and *fa* and between *ti* and _____.

DO

✠   ✠   ✠   ✠

To retain the distinctive pattern of whole and half steps in major scales other than C, it is necessary to use one or more of the black piano keys. An arrow points to the black key required in playing the G major scale from G to G.

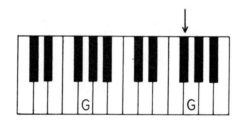

The notes played on the black keys are named and written as modified forms of the white-key notes. The note in the G major scale played on a black key is F-sharp. F-_____ is

SHARP

a half step higher than F.

F-sharp is written like F with a *sharp sign* in front of the note.

Sharp sign    ♯

A sharp sign raises the pitch a half step. Draw a sharp sign.

Sharp sign _____

♯

Provide the missing note names.

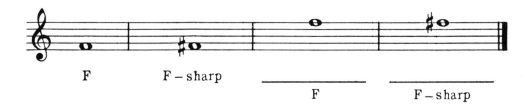

F          F – sharp          _____          _____
                                 F                 F – sharp

Observe that the sharp sign precedes the note on the staff but that the word *sharp* follows the letter name in speaking and writing. Write the specified notes on the staff.

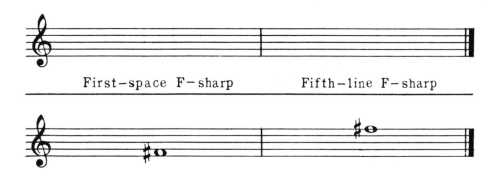

First – space  F – sharp          Fifth – line  F – sharp

F-sharp is a half step higher than _____. F-sharp is played on the black key above (to the right of) the F key. Draw arrows pointing to the F-sharp keys on the keyboard.

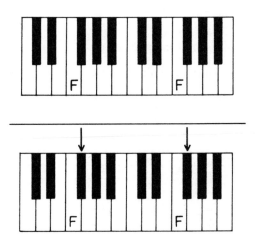

Add a sharp sign in front of the F to make this a G major scale.

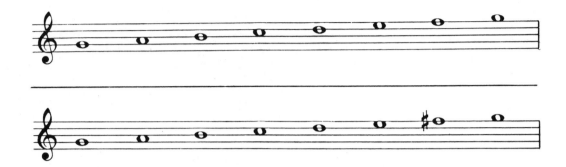

Draw arrows pointing to the keys used in playing a G major scale from G to G. Draw the arrows pointing up to white keys and down to black keys.

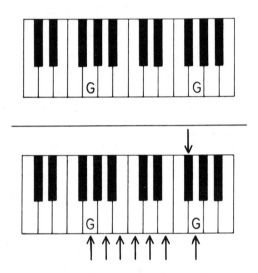

Play a G major scale ascending and descending.

Write the letter names of the G major scale under the notes. A sharp sign may be used in place of the word with the letter name, F♯ instead of F-sharp.

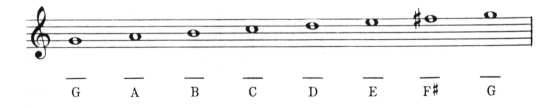

G    A    B    C    D    E    F♯    G

The number names of the notes in a major scale are the same no matter where it starts. The keynote is numbered 1, and the other notes are numbered consecutively up to the next keynote which is numbered 8 or 1 again. In the G major scale the keynote is _____, and the first G is numbered 1. Give the number names for the other notes of the G major scale.

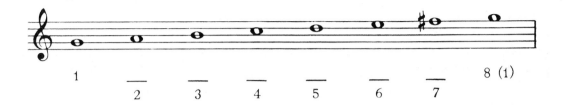

In a G major scale the letter name of the seventh scale degree is _____.
The syllable names, like the number names, are the same in all major scales. The keynote is always *do*. In the key of G major *do* is _____. Write the notes above the syllable names to make a G major scale.

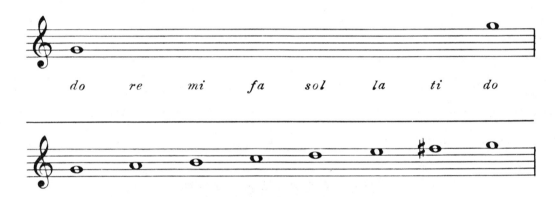

do    re    mi    fa    sol    la    ti    do

If you forgot to put a sharp sign on the F, go back and add it now.

Scale patterns, like letter names, are repeated in each octave throughout the entire range of the keyboard. The G major scale can begin or end on any G. The major scale pattern appears twice in the following example.

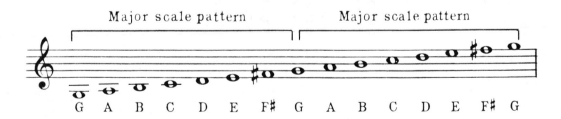

Major scale pattern        Major scale pattern

G    A    B    C    D    E    F♯    G    A    B    C    D    E    F♯    G

All of the notes in G major are used in the following version of *America*. It is in the key of G _____. It begins and ends on the keynote. The keynote is _____.

The two F's in the melody are sharped. Write the letter names below the notes. Add a sharp sign to the letter name of the F-sharps.

America

G G A F# G A B B C B A G A G F# G D D D

D C B C C C C B A B C B A G B C D E C B A G

Sing *America* substituting the letter names of the notes for the words.

An arrow points to the location of the keynote on which the melody of *America* begins and ends. Draw arrows pointing to the location on the keyboard of the other notes in the melody. As always, draw arrows up to white keys and down to black keys.

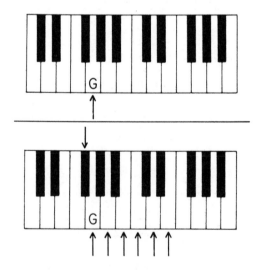

Reading from the notation, play *America* on the piano or locate the notes rhythmically on the tear-out keyboard while humming the melody.

Sharps which are used consistently are written on the staff as a *key signature* at the beginning of each line. Each key _____ SIGNATURE is associated with a particular major key. The

_____ KEY signature for G major is one sharp written on the fifth (top) line.

Key signature for G major

The fifth line in the treble clef is F. When a sharp is written on the F line as a key _____, SIGNATURE the F's in all octaves are sharp unless otherwise indicated.

The key signature for G major is one _____ SHARP. This sharp is on the _____ FIFTH (TOP) line. Write the key signature for G major on the treble staff.

The key signature for *America* in the key of G major is one sharp on fifth-line F. The sharp on the fifth line makes all of the F's _____ SHARP, including first-space F's. The first phrase of *America* is written in the key of G with a key signature. Write a sharp sign below the notes which are made sharp by the key signature.

America

Observe that the key signature comes between the clef sign and the time signature.

✠   ✠   ✠   ✠

All of the notes played on the black keys of the piano can be written as sharps. Each black key takes its sharp name from the white key on its left. The sharp letter names are written above the black keys in one octave of the keyboard diagram. Write the sharp letter names above the black keys in the other octave.

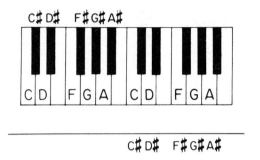

A sharp raises the pitch a half step.

C-sharp is a half step higher than —————————.
C

D-sharp is a half step higher than —————————.
D

F-sharp is a half step higher than —————————.
F

G-sharp is a half step higher than —————————.
G

A-sharp is a half step higher than —————————.
A

These five notes with and without sharps are located on the staff and on the keyboard as follows:

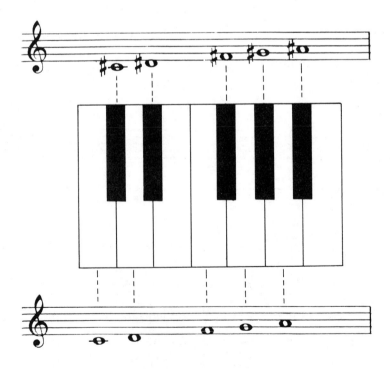

Sharp notes occur in all octaves. Name these sharp notes.

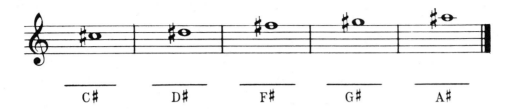

C♯    D♯    F♯    G♯    A♯

Sharp notes are used in various combinations in certain major scales and keys. F-sharp and C-sharp are used in the D major scale and in the key of D _____. Draw arrows MAJOR pointing to the F-sharps and C-sharps on the keyboard.

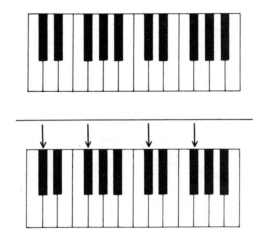

The key signature for D major is two sharps, F-sharp and C-sharp, in that order.

Key signature for D major

In the D major key signature the first sharp, F-sharp, is written on the fifth _____. LINE The second sharp, C-sharp, is written in the third _____. Write the key signature SPACE for D major on the staff.

*Prayer of Thanksgiving* is in the key of D major. In the key signature of D major there are two sharps, F-sharp and ———————————. Write sharp signs below all of the notes in the melody
<sub>C-SHARP</sub>
which are raised by the sharps in the key signature.

### Prayer of Thanksgiving

All of the notes from D below the staff to E in the fourth space are used in *Prayer of Thanksgiving*. Draw arrows pointing to all of the keys used in playing the melody. Remember the sharps in the key signature.

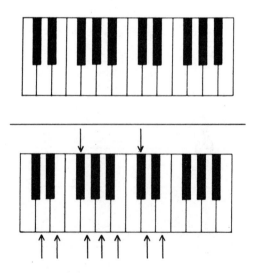

If you know the melody of *Prayer of Thanksgiving,* hum it as you point to the keys used in playing it. If the melody is unfamiliar, play it slowly on the piano.

Whenever you have difficulty reading rhythms and pitches at the same time, practice the rhythm independently as you did in the rhythm studies in the first part of the book.

As an aid in locating notes on the keyboard, write the letter names on the white keys and above the notes in the music. After the marks have served their purpose, they can be erased.

The key signature for D major is two sharps, F-sharp and C-sharp. For the key of A major, a third sharp is added. The third sharp in a sharp key signature is G-sharp.

Key signature for A major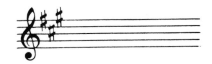

A key signature of two sharps is printed on the following staff. This is the signature for _____ major. Add a third sharp to make the signature for A major. The third sharp

D

goes above the fifth line.

In the next example an A major scale is written with a key signature. Write a sharp sign below each note of the scale raised by a sharp in the signature.

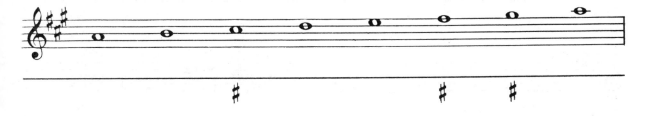

Draw arrows pointing to the keys used in playing an A major scale from A to A an octave higher.

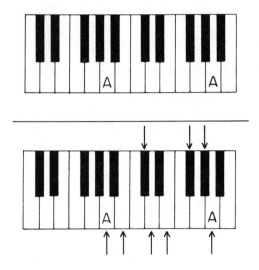

Play the A major scale ascending and descending.

In the key signature of A major there are three _____. These sharps are, in

SHARPS

order of their appearance, F-sharp, C-sharp, and _____.

G-SHARP

*Flow Gently, Sweet Afton* is in the key of A major. Write sharp signs under the notes of the

melody which are raised by the sharps in the key signature.

Flow Gently, Sweet Afton

Did you write sharp signs under all of the notes raised by the sharps in the signature? If not, add them now. Remember, the sharp on the fifth line applies to all F's. Likewise, the sharp above the fifth line applies to all ⎯⎯⎯⎯⎯⎯⎯⎯⎯.
G's

Play *Flow Gently, Sweet Afton* on the piano or locate the notes on the tear-out keyboard while humming the melody.

The signature for the key of E major is four sharps. The first three sharps are the same as for A major—F-sharp, C-sharp, and ⎯⎯⎯⎯⎯⎯⎯⎯⎯. The fourth sharp is D-sharp, written on the
G-SHARP
fourth line in the treble clef.

Key signature for E major

Add the fourth sharp to make an E major key signature.

Write a sharp below each note of the E major scale raised by a sharp in the key signature.

The sharps in the key of E major are F-sharp, C-sharp, G-sharp, and ⎯⎯⎯⎯⎯⎯⎯⎯⎯.
D-SHARP
These notes are played on the black keys of the piano. Draw arrows pointing to all of the black keys used in the key of E major.

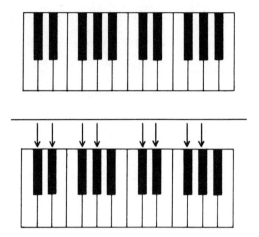

Did you draw arrows pointing to eight keys? Each of the four sharp notes in the key of E major appears twice in the keyboard diagram.

The key signature for B major is five sharps. The fifth sharp, A-sharp, is written in the second space of the treble staff. The other four sharps are the same as for the key of _____ major.

E

Key signature for B major

Referring to the B major key signature, write the letter names of the first five sharps in order of their appearance in sharp key signatures. Add a sharp sign to each letter name.

1. _____   2. _____   3. _____   4. _____   5. _____
   F#            C#            G#            D#            A#

Write these five sharps on the staff under the numbers in order of their appearance in sharp key signatures.

Write sharps below the notes raised by the sharps of the key signature in a two-octave B major scale.

Draw arrows pointing to all of the black keys used in the key of B major.

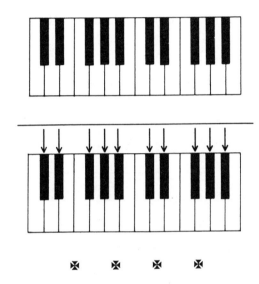

All of the pitches played on the black keys of the piano can be notated as sharp notes. The pitches played on the black keys of the piano can also be notated as *flat* notes. Flat notes are indicated by _____ signs.

FLAT

Flat sign    ♭

A flat sign lowers the pitch a half step. Write a flat sign.

Flat sign _____

♭

A sharp sign raises the pitch a half step. A flat sign _____ the pitch a half step.

LOWERS

Notes which are neither sharp nor flat are *natural*. Unless a sharp or flat applies, all notes are

_____. A natural sign cancels a sharp or a flat.

NATURAL

Natural sign ♮

A natural sign on a note cancels a sharp or flat in the key signature for the remainder of the measure. A natural sign also cancels any previous sharp or flat in the measure on the same note. Draw a natural sign.

Natural sign _____

♮

Sharps, flats, and naturals written on individual notes (not in key signatures) are *accidentals*. Write the specified accidentals.

Sharp _____ Flat _____ Natural _____

♯ ♭ ♮

A sharp or a flat written on a note is an _____. A natural on a note which is a

ACCIDENTAL

sharp or a flat in the key signature is also an _____. Accidentals apply only for the

ACCIDENTAL

remainder of the measure in which they appear and have no force beyond a bar line.

Sharp notes and flat notes are named and written as modified forms of natural notes. B-flat

is written like B with a _____ sign in front of the note.

FLAT

B          B−flat

Add flat signs as necessary to notate the specified pitches.

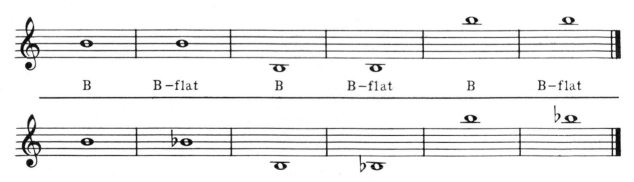

B          B−flat          B          B−flat          B          B−flat

Observe that flat signs, like sharp signs, precede the notes on the staff. The sign or word follows the letter name, B♭ or B-flat, in speaking and writing.

B-flat is a half step lower than —————————————. B-flats are played on the black keys below
(to the left of) the B keys.

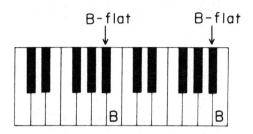

A-flat is a half step lower than ————————————. A-flats are played on the black keys below (to the left of) the A keys. Draw arrows pointing to the A-flat keys.

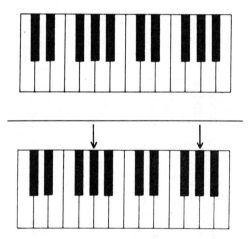

G-flat is a half step ———————————— than G. G-flats are played on the black keys below
(to the left of) the ———————————— keys. Draw arrows pointing to the G-flat keys.

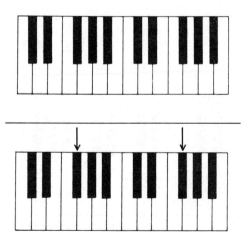

The note a half step lower than E is _____. E-flats are played on the black keys below (to the left of) the _____ keys. Draw arrows pointing to the E-flat keys.

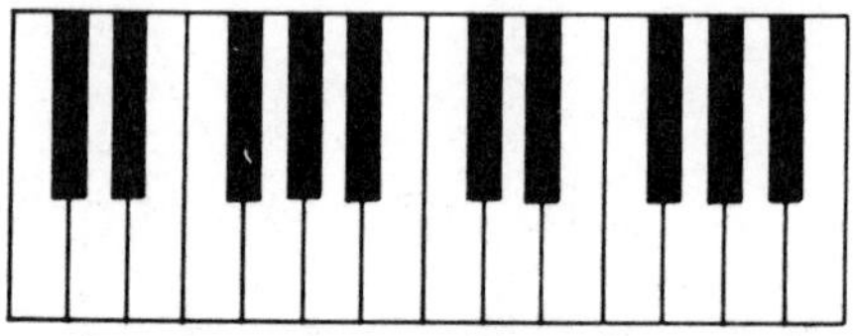

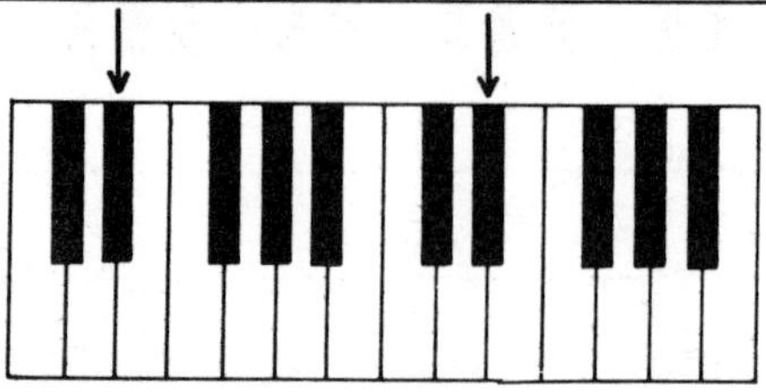

E-FLAT

E

The note played on the black key below D is _____. D-flat is a half step lower than _____. Draw arrows pointing to the D-flat keys.

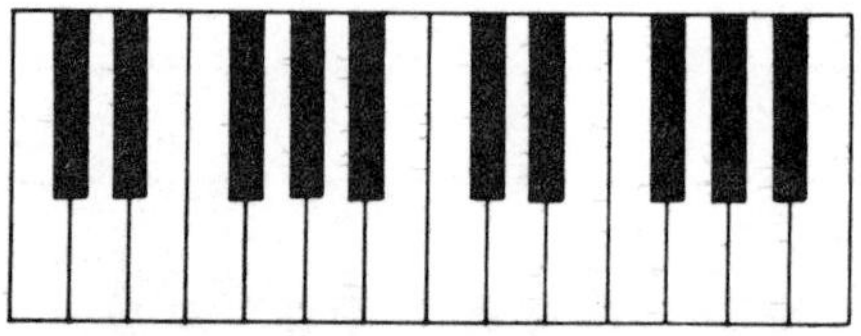

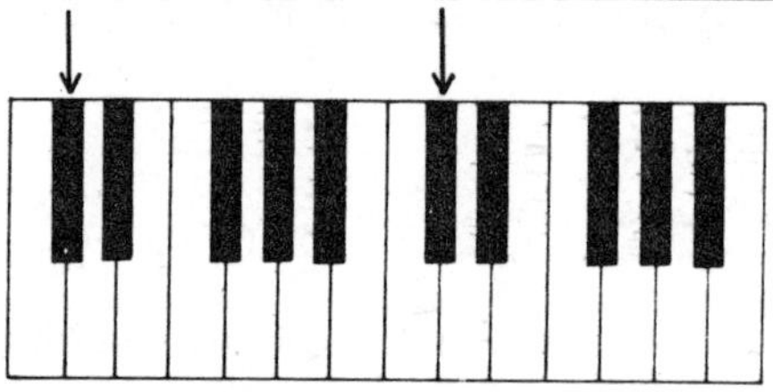

D-FLAT

D

All of the notes played on the black keys of the piano can be written as flats. Each black key takes its flat name from the white key on its right. The flat letter names are written above the black keys in one octave of the keyboard diagram. Write the flat letter names in the other octave.

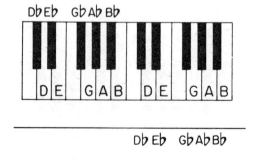

Db Eb  Gb Ab Bb

D E  G A B   D E  G A B

Db Eb  Gb Ab Bb

The five flat notes played on the black keys and the five natural notes with the same letter names are located on the staff and on the keyboard as follows:

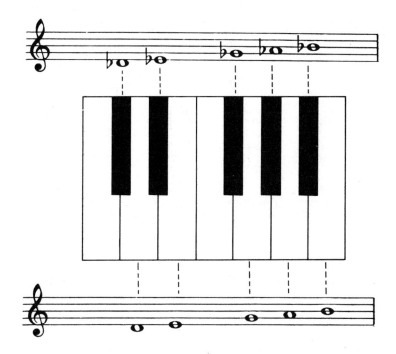

Flat notes occur in all octaves. Name these flat notes.

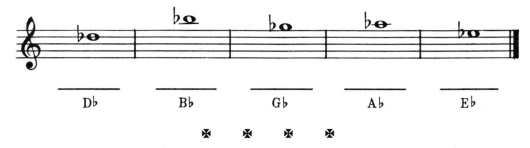

Db       Bb       Gb       Ab       Eb

✠     ✠     ✠     ✠

Flats are required in constructing several major scales. This is an F major scale. Write the letter names under the notes.

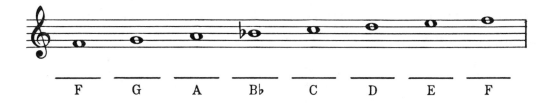

F     G     A     Bb     C     D     E     F

Play the F major scale from F to F. Be sure to play B-flat, not B. If you play a wrong note in a major scale, the sound will be strange.

Since B-flat is the one flat required in the F major scale, B-flat written on the third line is the key signature for the key of _____ major.
F

Key signature for F major

The same melody can be written in different keys. *America,* which is in the key of G major on page 80, can also be written in the key of F major. When the key is F major, the key signature is one _____ on the third line. The following version of *America* is in the key of F major.
FLAT
Write the letter names below the notes adding flat signs to all B's, which are flatted by the B-flat in the key signature.

America

Sing *America* in the key of F major with the letter names. Draw arrows pointing to the keys used in playing *America* in F major starting from the F marked on the keyboard. Remember the B-flat in the signature.

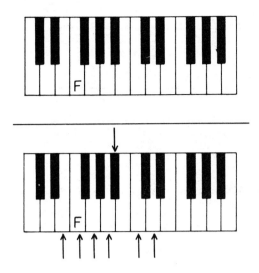

Return to the notation of *America* in the key of **F** major and play the melody on the piano or locate the notes rhythmically on the tear-out keyboard while humming the melody.

Some scales begin on flat notes. The following is a B-flat major scale. A B-flat major scale begins and ends on _____. The keynote is _____. Write the letter names,
 <sub>B-FLAT</sub>                              <sub>B-FLAT</sub>
with flat signs as appropriate, under the notes of the B-flat major scale.

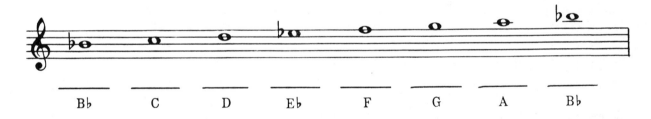

Bb      C      D      Eb      F      G      A      Bb

In the key signature of B-flat major there are two _____.
FLATS

Key signature for B-flat major

In the key signature for B-flat major the first flat is B-flat. The second flat is _____.
E-FLAT
The B-flat goes on the third _____. The E-flat goes in the fourth _____.
LINE                                    SPACE
Write the key signature for B-flat major on the staff.

*Yale Boola* is in the key of B-flat major. Write the letter names, with flat signs as appropriate, under the notes.

Yale Boola

D  E♭  F  D    C  D  B♭  F    G  F  F  A    G  F  F  B♭

D  E♭  F  D    C  D  B♭  F    G  F  F  A    G  F  B♭

Sing *Yale Boola* with the letter names.

Locate the notes of *Yale Boola* on the tear-out keyboard while humming the melody, or play the melody on the piano.

The key of E-flat major has a signature of three _____. The third flat, A-flat, is added to the B-flat and E-flat used in a key signature of two flats. Write flat signs below the notes of an E-flat major scale which are lowered by the flats in the key signature.

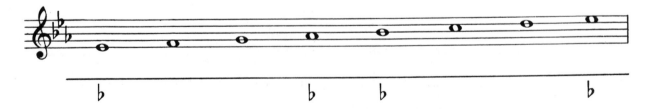

Did you write flat signs below both E-flats? Remember, a flat in the signature applies to the note of that letter name in all octaves.

Add a third flat to the following key signature to make the signature for E-flat major.

In flat key signatures, the first flat is _____; the second flat is _____;
B-FLAT                                                        E-FLAT
and the third flat is _____. The major key with three flats in its signature is
A-FLAT
_____ major.
E-FLAT

*When the Saints Go Marching In* is in the key of E-flat major. Write the letter names under the

notes of the melody.

When the Saints Go Marching In

Did you add flats to the letter names of notes which are flats in the key signature? For the

pitches indicated by the letter names to correspond with those written on the staff, the flat sign must

be added to all B's, E's, and _____.
A's

Go back to the notation of *When the Saints Go Marching In* and sing it with letter names. (Saying "flat" with the letter names of flat notes is not practical in a fast tempo.) Then hum the melody while you locate the notes on the tear-out keyboard or play them on a piano.

The key signature for A-flat major is four flats. The first three flats are the same as for E-flat major — B-flat, E-flat, and _____. The fourth flat, D-flat, is written on the fourth line of the treble staff.

A-FLAT

Key signature for A-flat major

Add a fourth flat to make the key signature for A-flat major.

Write flats below all of the notes affected by the key signature in a two-octave A-flat major scale.

Draw arrows pointing to all of the black keys used in the key of A-flat major.

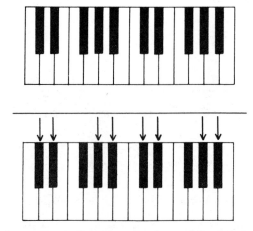

The key signature for D-flat major is five flats. In the treble clef the fifth flat, G-flat, is written on the second line.

Key signature for D-flat major

Referring to the D-flat major key signature, write the letter names of the first five flats in order of their appearance in flat key signatures. Add a flat sign to each letter name.

1. _____ B♭    2. _____ E♭    3. _____ A♭    4. _____ D♭    5. _____ G♭

Write these five flats on the staff under the numbers in order of their appearance in flat key signatures.

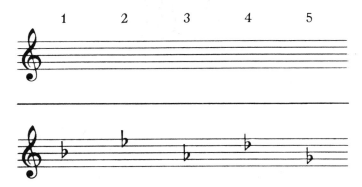

Write flats below all of the notes affected by the key signature in a two-octave D-flat major scale.

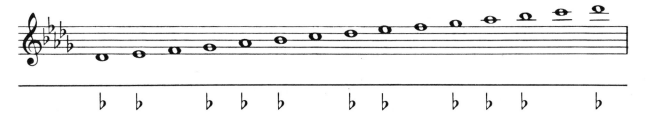

Draw arrows pointing to all of the black keys used in the key of D-flat major.

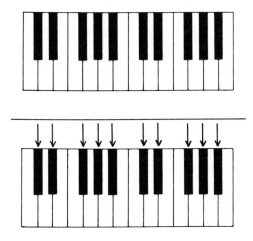

Observe that all five black **keys** in an octave are used in D-flat major. Write the flat letter names above the black keys.

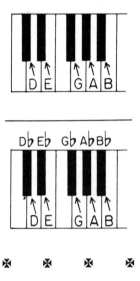

All five black keys are also used in the key of B major, which has a signature of five sharps. The sharp letter names, you will remember, are the same letter as the white key on the left. Write the sharp letter names above the black keys.

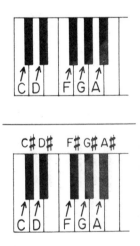

Compare the two previous examples which show the flat letter names and the sharp letter names for the black keys. It is apparent that each black key serves for two notes, a sharp note and a flat note. Write the sharp letter name and the flat letter name above each black key.

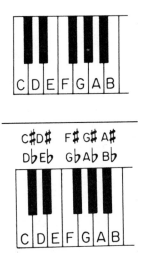

Study every feature of the following example to help clarify some of the most perplexing aspects of music notation. Notes and letter names without a sharp or flat sign are natural. Notes with the same pitch are aligned vertically with each other and with the piano key on which they are played.

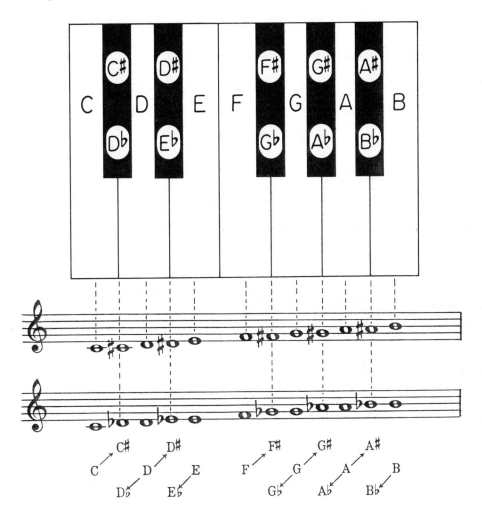

Each black key serves for a sharp note and a flat note. The pairs of notes played on the same black key are:

C-sharp and _____
D-FLAT

D-sharp and _____
E-FLAT

F-sharp and _____
G-FLAT

G-sharp and _____
A-FLAT

A-sharp and _____
B-FLAT

Notes which are played on the same key have the same sound. Notes which have the same sound but which are written differently and have different letter names are *enharmonic* notes. Complete the following list of _____ notes.
ENHARMONIC

D-flat is the enharmonic equivalent of _____.
C-SHARP

E-flat is the enharmonic equivalent of _____.
D-SHARP

G-flat is the enharmonic equivalent of _____.
F-SHARP

A-flat is the enharmonic equivalent of _____.
G-SHARP

B-flat is the enharmonic equivalent of _____.
A-SHARP

✠　　✠　　✠　　✠

A scale which includes every pitch, those played on the black keys as well as those played on the white keys, is a *chromatic* scale. An ascending _____ scale is written using natural
CHROMATIC
and sharp notes. Write the letter names under the notes of the ascending chromatic scale.

C　C♯　D　D♯　E　F　F♯　G　G♯　A　A♯　B　C

Locate the notes of this chromatic scale on the keyboard and say the letter name of each note as you play or point to the key.

A descending chromatic scale is written using natural and flat notes. Sharps are used for ascending chromatic scales and flats for descending _____ scales. Write the letter
CHROMATIC
names under the notes of this descending chromatic _____.
SCALE

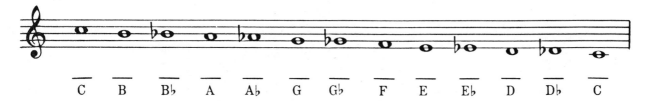

C   B   B♭   A   A♭   G   G♭   F   E   E♭   D   D♭   C

Say the letter names of the notes in this descending chromatic scale as you locate them on the keyboard.

✠   ✠   ✠   ✠

Any note can be raised a half step by a sharp, including E and B, which have not been sharped previously. E-sharp is a half step higher than _____. F is also a half step higher than

_____. E-sharp and F are enharmonic notes. Enharmonic notes are played on the same key of the piano. E-sharp is played on the same key of the piano as _____.

Two E-sharps are written on the staff. Draw arrows pointing to their location on the keyboard.

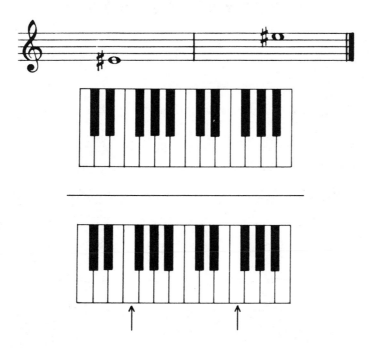

B-sharp and C are enharmonic notes. Write the enharmonic equivalent of each B-sharp in the blank measure following it.

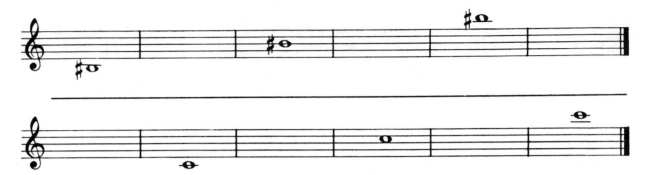

Draw an arrow pointing to the key near the center of the diagram used to play B-sharp.

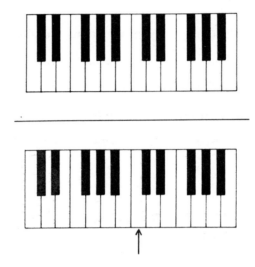

Any note can be lowered a half step by a flat, including C and F, which have not been flatted previously. Write the specified notes on the staff (no ledger lines).

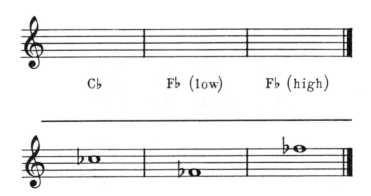

C♭          F♭ (low)          F♭ (high)

F-flat is the enharmonic equivalent of E and is played on the same key as _____.

E

Write the letter names on the two keys in the keyboard diagram used to play F-flats.

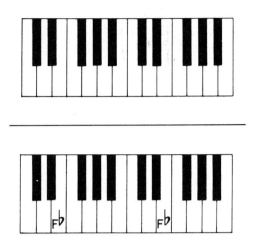

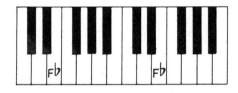

C-flat is the enharmonic equivalent of B and is played on the same key as _____.

Write the letter name on the C-flat key between the two F-flat keys in the keyboard diagram.

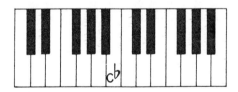

There is no black key between B and _____. There is no black key between E

and _____. The pairs of white keys which have no black key between them have

a sharp name or a flat name in addition to their natural name.

E-sharp, B-sharp, C-flat, and F-flat are used in keys with many sharps or flats in their signatures.

E-sharp is the sixth sharp in the key signature for F-sharp major. The sharps of the key signature are spread on the staff. Write the letter name under each sharp in the signature.

Key signature for F-sharp major

F♯    C♯    G♯    D♯    A♯    E♯

In the key of C-sharp major there are seven sharps in the signature. All of the notes are sharp. Write the letter names below the notes of the following C-sharp major scale.

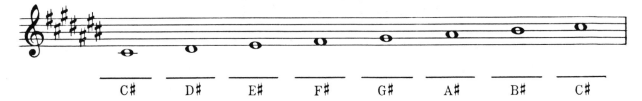

C♯    D♯    E♯    F♯    G♯    A♯    B♯    C♯

Draw arrows pointing to the notes of a C-sharp major scale between the two C-sharps marked on the keyboard. Remember, E-sharp is played on the same key as _____, and

<small>F</small>

B-sharp is played on the same key as _____.

<small>C</small>

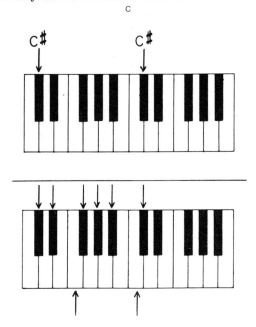

C-flat is the sixth flat in the key signature for G-flat major. The flats of the key signature are spread on the staff. Write the letter name below each flat in the signature.

Key signature for G-flat major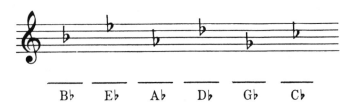

B♭    E♭    A♭    D♭    G♭    C♭

In the key of C-flat major there are seven flats in the signature. All of the notes are flat. Write the letter names below the notes of the following C-flat major scale.

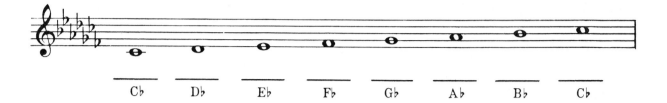

| C♭ | D♭ | E♭ | F♭ | G♭ | A♭ | B♭ | C♭ |

Draw arrows pointing to the notes of a C-flat major scale between the two C-flats marked on the keyboard. C-flat, on which the scale begins and ends, is played on the same key as _____.

B

F-flat is played on the same key as _____.

E

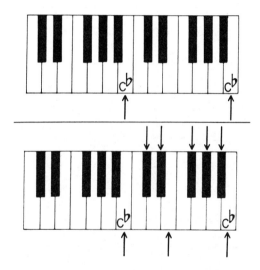

Keys with many sharps or flats are used infrequently, because playing in these keys is difficult on most instruments.

✠     ✠     ✠     ✠

Each type of scale has a distinctive pattern of intervals. The intervals between consecutive degrees of major scales are whole steps and _____ steps.

HALF

When the degrees of a major scale are numbered from 1 to 8, the half steps are between 3 and 4 and between 7 and 8. The intervals between other consecutive degrees are _____ steps.

WHOLE

Scales are identified by the letter name of the note on which they begin and end. The type of scale is indicated by a word like *major*. The following example shows how a C major scale is written and played. The scale degrees are numbered, and the half steps are marked.

### C Major Scale

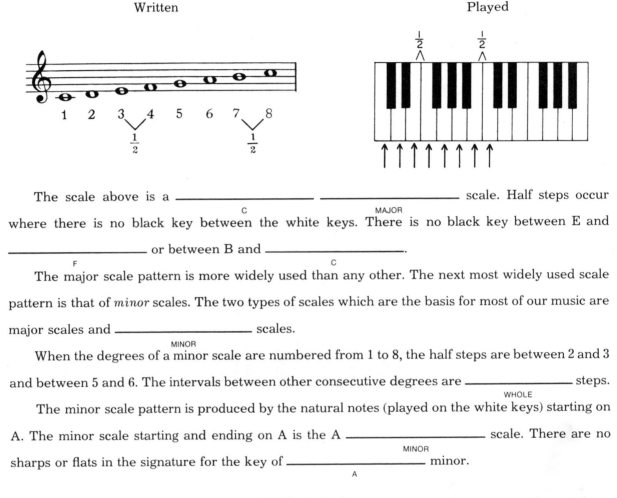

The scale above is a _____ _____ scale. Half steps occur

where there is no black key between the white keys. There is no black key between E and

_____ or between B and _____ .

The major scale pattern is more widely used than any other. The next most widely used scale

pattern is that of *minor* scales. The two types of scales which are the basis for most of our music are

major scales and _____ scales.

When the degrees of a minor scale are numbered from 1 to 8, the half steps are between 2 and 3

and between 5 and 6. The intervals between other consecutive degrees are _____ steps.

The minor scale pattern is produced by the natural notes (played on the white keys) starting on

A. The minor scale starting and ending on A is the A _____ scale. There are no

sharps or flats in the signature for the key of _____ minor.

### A Minor Scale

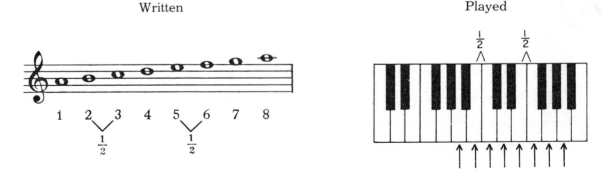

In the A minor scale half steps occur where there is no black key between the white keys. Half steps in the A minor scale are between B and _____ (C) and between E and _____ (F). In minor scales the half steps are between scale degrees 2 and _____ (3) and between scale degrees 5 and _____ (6). The intervals between other consecutive degrees of minor scales are _____ (WHOLE) steps.

The following portion of *We Three Kings* uses all the notes in the key of A minor. It is in the key of _____ (A) minor. Sing or play the melody. Listen for the distinctive quality of minor and notice how different it sounds from major.

We Three Kings

*We Three Kings* is in the key of _____ (A) minor. It ends on the keynote, A. There are no sharps or flats in the key signature.

✠   ✠   ✠   ✠

Each key signature serves for two keys, one major key and one minor key. The major key with no sharps or flats in its signature is C major. The minor key with no sharps or flats in its signature is _____ (A) minor. The key of a piece with no sharps or flats in its signature is either _____ (C) major or _____ (A) minor.

To tell whether a piece is in a major key or a minor key, look at the last note. The last note of melodies, with few exceptions, is the *keynote*. In the key of C the keynote is _____ (C), and melodies ordinarily end on _____ (C). A piece which ends on C and has no sharps or flats in its signature is in the key of _____ (C) major.

In the key of A the keynote is _____ (A), and melodies ordinarily end on _____ (A). A piece which ends on A and has no sharps or flats in its signature is in the key of _____ (A) minor.

110

Key signature and keynote of C major*

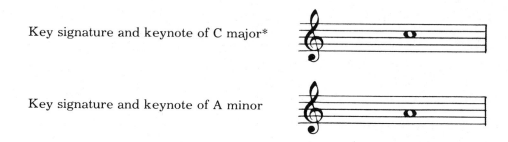

Key signature and keynote of A minor

[*Note: *The major key and the minor key which have the same signature are* relative *keys.* C major is the *relative major* of A minor. A minor is the *relative minor* of C major.]

The keynotes of the major key and the minor key with the same key signature are in consecutive spaces or on consecutive lines. When the keynote of a major key is in a space, the keynote of the minor key with the same key signature is in the next space below. When the keynote of a major key is on a line, the keynote of the minor key with the same key signature is on the next _____

LINE

below. If the keynote of C major is written in the third space, the keynote of A minor, which has the same key signature, is written in the second _____. If the keynote of C major is

SPACE

written an octave higher or an octave lower, it falls on a line, and the A below it also falls on a

_____.

LINE

Major keynotes:        C            C            C

Key signature: no
sharps or flats

Minor keynotes:        A            A            A

In sharp key signatures the last sharp comes between the major keynote and the minor keynote. The keys of G major and E minor have the same key signature, one sharp. The last (and only) sharp is written on the fifth line between E and G.

Major keynote, G

Key signature:
one sharp on F

Minor keynote, E

When the key signature is one sharp on F, the major keynote is the next note above, —————— ,
G

and the minor keynote is the next note below, —————— .
E

When the key signature is two sharps, the second (last) sharp is on C. The note above C is

—————— , so the major key with a signature of two sharps is —————— major.
D                                                                        D

The note below C is B, so the minor key with a signature of two sharps is —————— minor.
B

Major keynote, D

Key signature:
sharps on F and C

Minor keynote, B

If there is a sharp on the keynote in the key signature, the keynote is sharped. The sharp must

be stated in naming the keynote and the key.

Major keynote, A

Key signature:
sharps on F, C, and G

Minor keynote, F-sharp

Write the specified keynotes on the staff.

Major keynote, E

Key signature: sharps
on F, C, G, and D

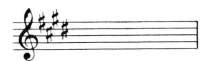

Minor keynote, C-sharp

—————————————————

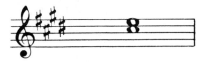

Study the following key signature and be prepared to answer questions about it.

How many sharps are there in the key signature? _____
7

What is the letter name of the last sharp? _____
B

What major key has this signature? _____
C-SHARP

What minor key has this signature? _____
A-SHARP

If you forgot to add *sharp* after the letter names of the keys in the previous questions, it was probably because you failed to observe the sharps in the key signature on both of the keynotes. The third sharp in the key signature is C-sharp, so the major key with seven sharps in the signature is C-_____ major. The fifth sharp in the signature is A-sharp, so the minor key
SHARP
with seven sharps in the signature is A-_____ minor. Remember, C major and A
SHARP
minor are the keys with no sharps or flats in their key signatures.

Name the minor key which has the following key signature and write its keynote on the staff.

G-sharp minor

Name the major key which has the following key signature and write its keynote on the staff.

F-sharp major

In keys with flat signatures the *last flat,* the *minor keynote,* and the *major keynote* ascend in that order on three consecutive lines or in three consecutive spaces. Observe the operation of this principle in the next six examples.

Major keynote, F

Key signature:
one flat on B

Minor keynote, D

In the preceding example:

The one (last) flat is on the ———————————— line.
THIRD

The minor keynote is on the ———————————— line.
FOURTH

The major keynote is on the ———————————— line.
FIFTH

Major keynote, E-flat

Key signature:
flats on B, E, and A

Minor keynote, C

In the preceding example:

The last flat is in the ———————————— space.
SECOND

The minor keynote is in the ———————————— space.
THIRD

The major keynote is in the ———————————— space.
FOURTH

This system for finding the keynotes of flat key signatures works even if the keynotes are above the staff.

Key signature:
flats on B and E

114

When the key signature is two flats, as it is in the preceding example:

The last flat is _____.
E-FLAT

The minor keynote is _____.
G

The major keynote is _____.
B-FLAT

When the key signature is five flats, the last flat is on the second line. Write the minor and major keynotes on the staff.

When the key signature is five flats, as it is in the preceding example, the major keynote is

_____, and the minor keynote is _____. Did you remember that
D-FLAT                                          B-FLAT
D and B are flats in the key signature and that the major keynote is above the minor keynote?

Write the minor keynote on the staff and name the minor key for the following key signature.

F minor

Write the major keynote on the staff and name the major key for the following key signature.

A-flat major

The major keynote can be verified by comparing it with the next-to-last flat. The next-to-last flat and the major keynote are always the same.

Major keynote, A-flat

Next-to-last flat, A-flat

To tell whether a piece with a flat key signature is in a major key or a minor key, follow the same procedure as for sharp key signatures and for the signature without sharps or flats. It is safe to assume that the last note of a melody is the ———————————. Notes other than the keynote are
                                                          KEYNOTE
unsuitable for endings under ordinary circumstances. A key signature of one flat on the third line (B-flat) indicates the key of F major or the key of D minor. If the last note of the melody is F, the keynote is ———————————, and the key of the piece is F ———————————. If the last note
                    F                                                 MAJOR
of the melody is D, the keynote is ———————————, and the key of the piece is D ———————————.
                                              D                                                 MINOR

Sometimes capital letters are used to indicate major keys, and small (lower case) letters are used to indicate minor keys. When this is done, the capital letter by itself means that the key is major, and the small letter by itself means that the key is ———————————. Observing this principle,
                                                                      MINOR
give a single letter name for the following keys:

E major = ———————————
                      E
E minor = ———————————
                      e

When the key name includes a sharp or a flat, the appropriate symbol is added to the letter name. Write out the full name of the keys indicated by these letters and signs.

E♭ = ——————————— ———————————
            E-FLAT                    MAJOR
c♯ = ——————————— ———————————
            C-SHARP                   MINOR

When the words *major* and *minor* are used with the letter names to identify keys, it is customary to use capital letters for both major and minor keys.

In minor keys and scales the sixth and seventh degrees are frequently raised by a sharp or, in flat keys, by a natural. The raised sixth and seventh degrees in minor correspond to the sixth and seventh degrees of the major key and scale with the same keynote. The raised sixth and seventh degrees in minor are, in effect, borrowed from the major key with the same keynote.

The keys of A major and A minor have the same keynote. The notes from A major used in A minor (which has no sharps in its signature) are F-sharp and G-sharp. Various forms of A minor are created by substituting F-sharp for F-natural and/or G-sharp for G-natural. The sharps in the key of A minor are always written as accidentals on individual notes, never added to the key signature.

The sharps from A major used in A minor are enclosed in parentheses in the following notation of the A minor scale. Draw arrows pointing to the location of the two sharp notes on the keyboard.

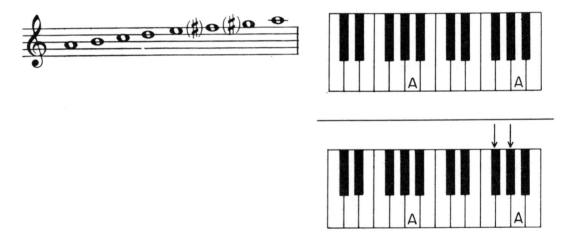

The sixth degree of an A minor scale may be either F-natural or F-sharp, but not both. The seventh degree may be either G-natural or G-sharp, but not both. Each form of a minor scale has only seven different notes, eight counting the repetition of the keynote. Compositions in minor keys, however, sometimes use both the regular and the borrowed notes. In *Go Down, Moses*, for example, there are several G-sharps and one G-natural. The sharp signs apply to the G's on which they are written and to the repetitions of that note within the measure, but not to G's in other measures. The G with the natural sign would be natural anyway, but the sign serves as a safeguard against misinterpretation.

Go Down, Moses

Give the letter names of the notes used in *Go Down, Moses* in order from low to high. The first note, E, is the lowest. List only notes which are used in the melody. Remember the two kinds of G's.

Did you list an F? If so, check the melody again. There are no F's in it.

Draw arrows pointing to the keys which would be used in playing *Go Down, Moses*.

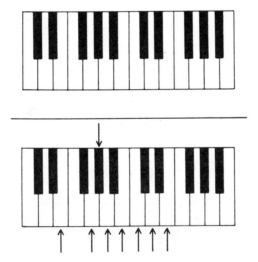

Sing or play *Go Down, Moses* being sure to distinguish between the G-sharps and the one G-natural. The song is in the key of A _____. It ends on the keynote, _____.
                                                    MINOR                                                         A
There are no sharps or flats in the key signature. The G-sharps are written as accidentals.

In some minor keys with flat signatures the notes borrowed from major are natural notes. In the key of C minor, which has three flats in its signature, A-natural and B-natural are used frequently. The C minor scale with the A-flat and the B-flat in the signature canceled by natural signs is placed beside the C major scale for comparison. Put an "x" under the notes that the two scales have in common.

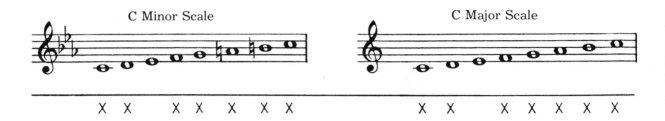

The third degree of the C major scale is _____. The third degree of the C minor

scale is _____. The critical difference between the two scales is in the third degree,

which is a half step higher in major than in minor. The other notes are used regularly in both C major

and C minor. What is true for C major and C minor is also true for all pairs of major and minor scales

with the same keynote.

Sharps and flats, except those in key signatures, are *accidentals.* Naturals which cancel sharps

or flats in key signatures are also *accidentals.* Notes other than those indicated by the key signature

are written as _____. Notes written as accidentals are *chromatic* notes. A scale

which contains all chromatic notes is a _____ scale.

The following melody contains several chromatic notes written as accidentals. An accidental

applies for the remainder of the measure in which it is written unless superseded by another acci-

dental. Only on tied notes does an accidental carry over a bar line. Write the letter names, with

accidentals as required, below the notes of the melody.

Sweet Genevieve

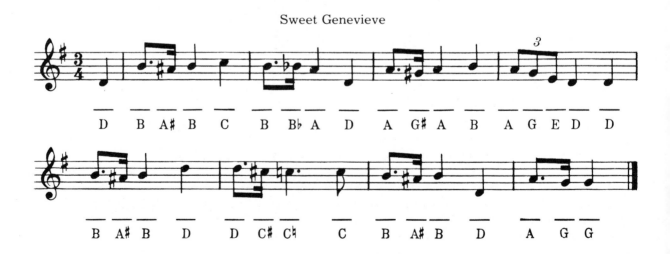

Practice singing or playing the melody and associating the notation of the chromatic notes with their sound.

✠ ✠ ✠ ✠

A *double sharp* occurs occasionally in keys (especially minor keys) with many sharps in the signature. A double ―――――――――― raises the pitch of a note which is already sharp an additional
SHARP
half step. A double sharp sign looks like an "x."

Double sharp sign ✗

Draw a double sharp sign.

Double sharp sign ――――――――――
✗

A double ―――――――――― raises the pitch of a note which is already sharp an additional
SHARP
half step. G-double-sharp is a half step higher than G-――――――――――. G-double-sharp is
SHARP
played on the next key above G-sharp.

G-sharp

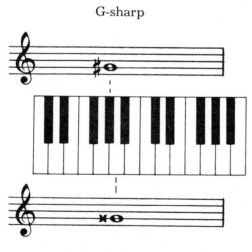

G-double-sharp

Observe that G-double-sharp is played on the same key as A. Notes which are written differently but have the same sound are *enharmonic* notes. G-double-sharp and A are ――――――――――
ENHARMONIC
notes.

Name the note and draw an arrow pointing to its location on the keyboard.

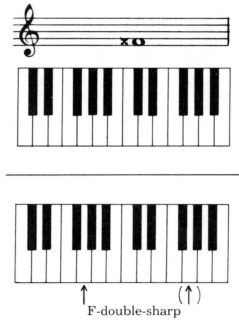

F-double-sharp

The flat equivalent of a double sharp is a *double flat*. A double flat lowers the pitch of a note which is already flat an additional half step. The name of the double flat sign is descriptive.

Double flat sign     ♭♭

Draw a double flat sign.

Double flat sign _____

♭♭

A double _____ lowers the pitch of a note which is already flat an additional
        FLAT
half step. B-double-flat is a half step lower than B-_____. B-double-flat is played
                           FLAT
on the next key below B-flat.

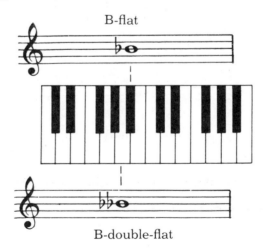

B-flat

B-double-flat

You will notice that B-double-flat is also played on the same key as A. B-double-flat is another enharmonic spelling for ————————————.

<sub>A</sub>

Name the note and draw an arrow pointing to its location on the keyboard.

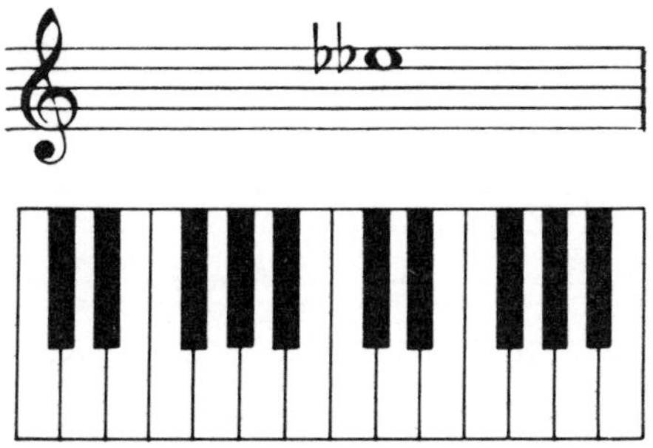

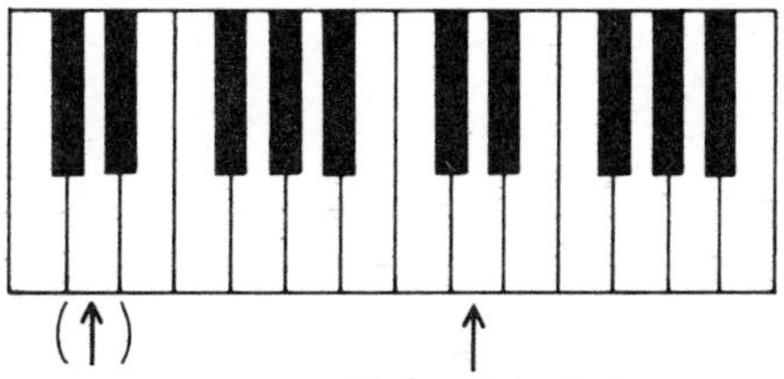

(↑)          ↑
     E-double-flat

Since double sharps and double flats are rare in the music of our time, they do not warrant further consideration at this level.

✠     ✠     ✠     ✠

Pitches too low to be notated conveniently in the treble clef are written in the *bass clef. Bass* in this usage is pronounced but NOT spelled like *base*. The sign on the following staff is a ———————————— clef sign.

BASS

Bass clef sign   𝄢

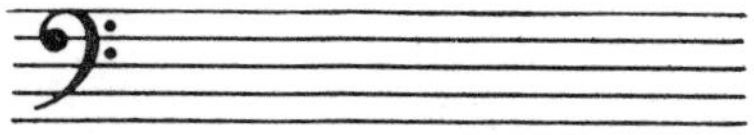

Draw a bass clef sign on each section of the staff. The two dots, one on each side of the fourth line, are essential features of the sign.

Typical manuscript symbols

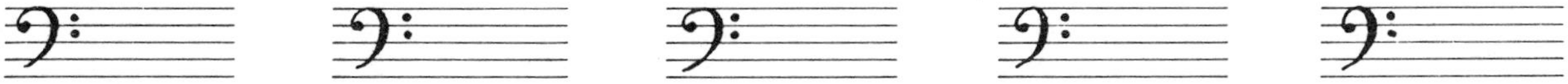

𝄢      𝄢      𝄢      𝄢      𝄢

The bass clef sign establishes a different set of meanings for the lines and spaces of the staff. The bass _____ is most easily explained as a continuation downward from the
CLEF
treble clef. A treble staff and a bass staff are joined to notate an extended range of pitches.

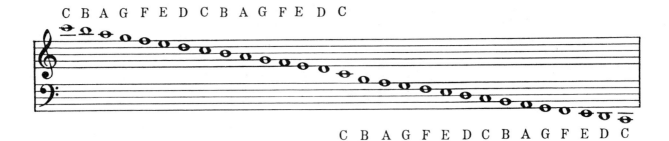

The note on the first ledger line below the treble staff is _____. The note on the
                                                                              C
first ledger line above the bass staff is also _____. This C, which is midway between
                                                              C
the treble staff and the bass staff and near the center of the piano keyboard, is *middle C*. Write middle C in both clefs.

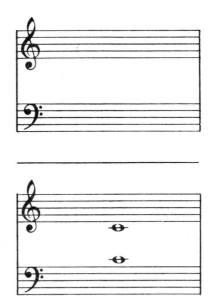

Write the missing letter names below the notes.

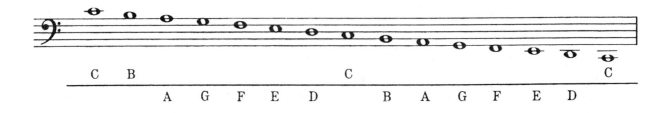

The letter names of the five lines in the bass clef can be associated with the initial letters of the words *Good Boys Do Fine Always.* Write the letter names below the notes on the five lines of the bass staff.

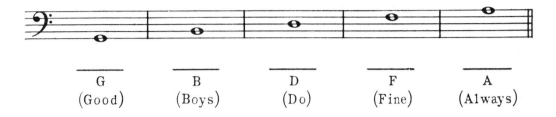

G      B      D      F      A

(Good)    (Boys)    (Do)    (Fine)    (Always)

The letter names of the four spaces in the bass clef can be associated with the initial letters of the words *All Cows Eat Grass.* Write the letter names below the notes in the four spaces of the bass staff.

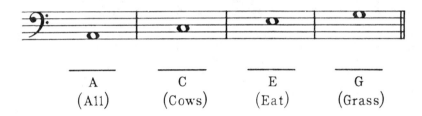

A      C      E      G

(All)    (Cows)    (Eat)    (Grass)

Name the note above and below the staff in the bass clef. When in doubt about the letter name of a note, start from a note you know and go forward or backward through the alphabet to the note in question.

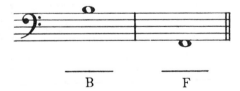

B      F

A treble staff and a bass staff are combined to notate music for keyboard instruments. Ordinarily, notes written in the treble clef are played with the right hand, and notes written in the bass clef are played with the left hand. The two staffs are joined, and bar lines extend from the top of the treble staff to the bottom of the bass staff. When ledger lines are used, the ranges of the two staffs overlap. Write the letter names above the notes in the bass clef and below the notes in the treble clef.

C D E F G A B C D E F G A B C D E F G A B C D E F G A B C

These notes are located on the keyboard as follows:

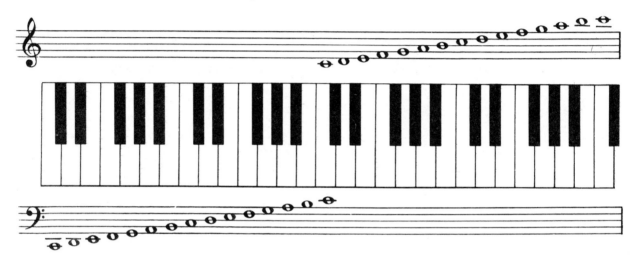

Draw arrows pointing to the location of the notes on the keyboard diagrams.

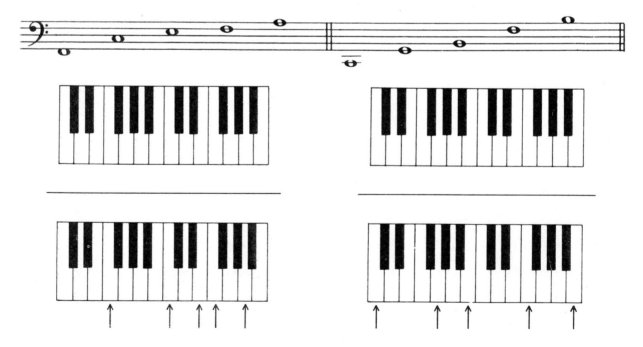

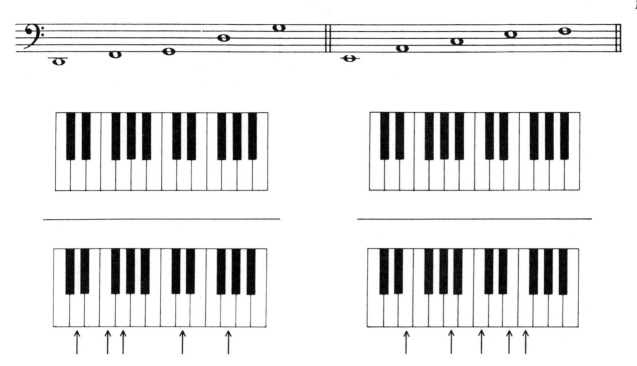

The melody of *Merrily We Roll Along* is written in the treble clef and an octave lower in the bass clef. Sing the melody with letter names, reading first from the treble clef and then from the bass clef. If a piano is available, play the treble part with the right hand and the bass part with the left hand, first separately and then together.

Merrily We Roll Along

E D C D  E E E  D D D  E G G  E D C D  E E E  D D E D  C

*Merrily We Roll Along* ends on C and is in the key of C _____.
<br>MAJOR

Write the letter names under the notes of *Good Night* and locate the notes on the keyboard with the left hand.

126

*Good Night*

*Good Night* is in the key of _____ _____.

<sub>C</sub> <sub>MAJOR</sub>

Sharps and flats function in the bass clef exactly as they do in the treble clef. A sharp raises the

pitch a _____ step. A flat _____ the pitch a half step. Sharps and

HALF                                                    LOWERS

flats are written on individual notes of the following melody to produce the proper pitches without

a key signature. Write the letter names, with sharp and flat signs as appropriate, below the notes.

Dark Eyes

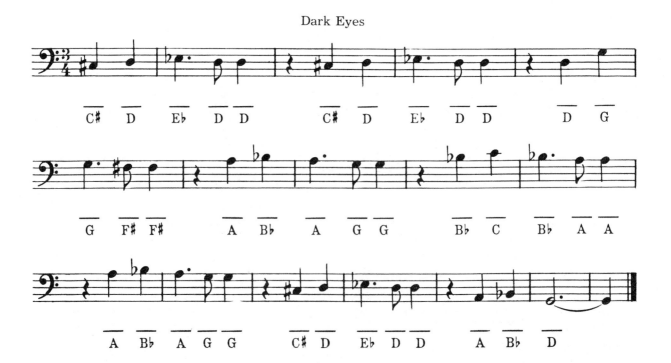

Sing *Dark Eyes* with *loo*, associating the notation with the sound.

Draw arrows pointing to the location of the following sharp and flat notes on the keyboard.

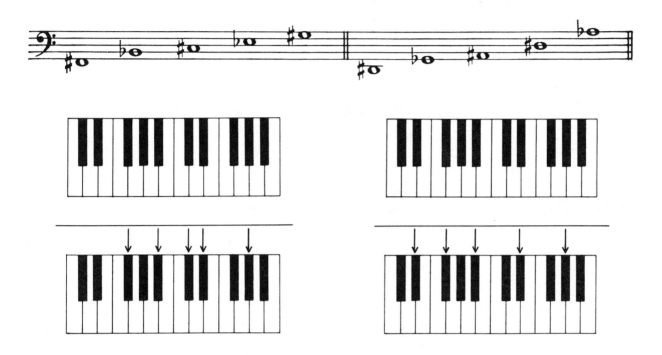

Key signatures are used in the bass clef as they are in the treble clef. The sharps and flats are added in the same order, but their location on the staff is different. Major and minor keynotes are determined in the same ways in the bass clef as they are in the treble clef. The sharp key signatures are given in both the treble and bass clefs, and the major and minor keynotes are given in the treble clef. Write the major and minor keynotes on the staff in the bass clef.

The key signature for *Are You Sleeping* is one sharp. The melody begins and ends on G. The song is in the key of G _____. It is written in a low octave to utilize the notes at the bottom of the bass staff. Write the letter names below the notes.

MAJOR

Are You Sleeping

G A B G    G A B G    B C D    B C D

D E D C B G    D E D C B G    G D G    G D G

Sing *Are You Sleeping* with letter names and locate the notes on the keyboard with the left hand. Observe that the key signature for G major is one sharp on F even when there is no F-sharp in the melody.

The keynotes for the following key signatures are written on the staff in the bass clef. Write the names of the major keys in capital letters above the staff and the names of the minor keys in small letters below the staff. Add a flat sign to the letter name of keynotes which are flat.

C    F    B♭    E♭    A♭    D♭    G♭    C♭

a    d    g    c    f    b♭    e♭    a♭

The key signature for *When Johnny Comes Marching Home* is two flats. The melody begins and ends on G. The song is in the key of G _____. In this key and octave several melody

MINOR

notes are above the fifth line of the bass clef. Write the letter names below these notes, adding a flat to the letter when a flat in the key signature applies.

When Johnny Comes Marching Home

One note in *When Johnny Comes Marching Home*, which is in the key of G minor, is borrowed from the key of G major. This note is ———————————.
F-SHARP

✠    ✠    ✠    ✠

An "8" over a note in the treble clef indicates that the note is to be played an octave *higher* than written. When a broken line extends from the number, all of the notes under the line are played an octave ——————————— than written. The *octave sign* reduces the number of ledger lines
HIGHER
required to write high notes. The notes are aligned with the keys on which they are played in the following example.

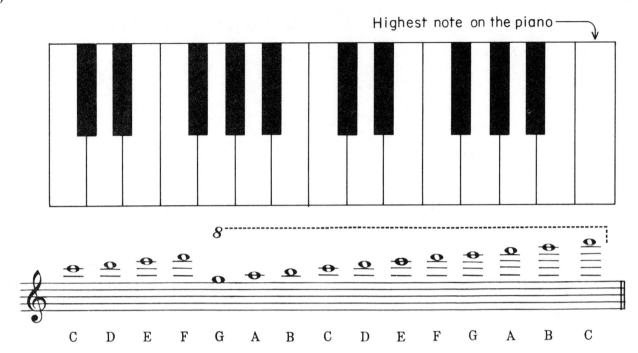

Locate the notes of the preceding example on the keyboard. The first note under the octave sign is a step higher than the note it follows, and the pitches continue on up to the highest note on the piano.

An "8" below a note in the bass clef indicates that the note is to be played an octave *lower* than written. When a broken line extends from the number, all of the notes above the line are to be played an octave _____ than written. An *octave sign* below the bass clef reduces the

LOWER

number of ledger lines required to write low notes. The notes are aligned with the keys on which they are played in the following example.

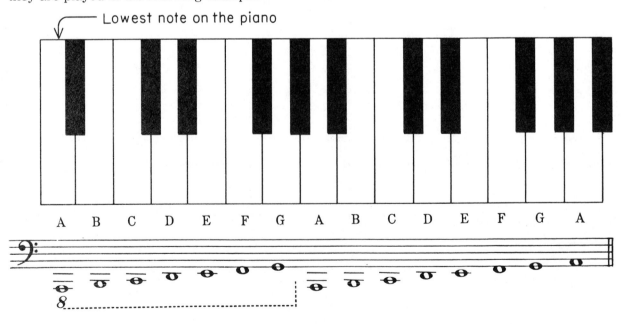

Locate the notes of the preceding example starting with the lowest note on the piano. The pitches continue to ascend by steps at the end of the octave sign.

✠    ✠    ✠    ✠

The pitch relationship between two notes is an *interval*. The _____ between two notes of the same pitch is a *unison*. The interval between two instruments playing the same note

INTERVAL

is a _____. When two or more voices sing the same melody at the same time, they

UNISON

are singing *in unison*. The word *unison* is derived from a word meaning *one*.

The names of the other intervals are also derived from numbers. In order from small to large, the names of the intervals are: *unison, second, third, fourth,* _____, *sixth,* _____,

FIFTH                    SEVENTH

and *octave*. Beyond an octave the interval names may start over like the letter names or may continue—*ninth, tenth,* etc. Numbering the notes and naming the intervals shows the relationship between the numbers and the interval names.

Intervals Above C

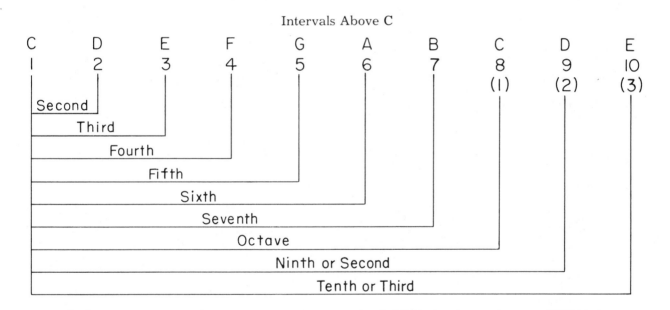

Another way of arriving at the interval names is to count the two notes and the lines and spaces between them on the staff.

Intervals Above C

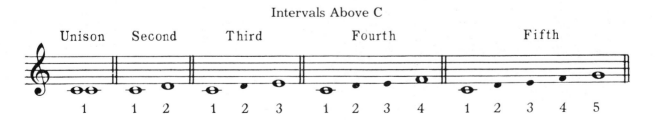

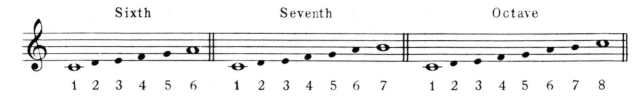

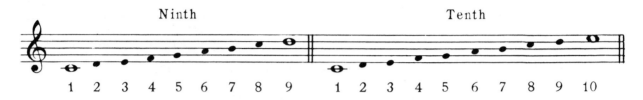

The interval between any two notes can be determined by this method. Use it to name the following intervals.

In naming intervals it makes no difference whether you start from the lower note or the higher note. Name these descending intervals.

The exact size of an interval varies with its location on the staff and with the key signature. The size can be modified by accidentals. The words added to the basic interval names to show exact size or *quality* are: *major, minor, perfect, augmented,* and *diminished.* The intervals above C are perfect or major as shown.

Unisons, fourths, fifths, and octaves may be *perfect, augmented,* or *diminished.* A half step larger than perfect is *augmented.* An interval is made larger by raising the top note or lowering the bottom note. Supply the interval name which is missing.

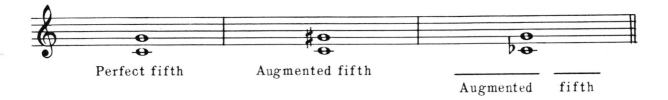

Unisons, fourths, fifths, and octaves may be *perfect, augmented,* or *diminished.* A half step smaller than perfect is *diminished.* An interval is made smaller by raising the bottom note or lowering the top note. Supply the interval name which is missing.

Seconds, thirds, sixths, and sevenths are usually *major* or *minor.* Major is a half step larger than minor. Minor is a half step smaller than _____.  An interval is made smaller by
<br>MAJOR
raising the bottom note or lowering the top note. Supply the interval name which is missing.

The interval between the keynote and the third degree of a major scale is a *major third.* In a C major scale the keynote is _____, and the third degree is E (natural). The interval
<br>C
between C and E is a major _____.
<br>THIRD
The interval between the keynote and the third degree of a minor scale is a *minor third.* In a C minor scale the keynote is _____, and the third degree is E-flat. The interval
<br>C
between C and E-flat is a minor _____.
<br>THIRD

✠    ✠    ✠    ✠

This completes the study of pitch notation. Now you should be able to read music in the treble and bass clefs and to sing and pick out on the piano songs of your choice. It takes extensive practice, of course, to develop reading proficiency and technical skill on an instrument.

The terms and symbols which remain to be learned supplement the rhythm and pitch symbols in the notation and interpretation of music.

# supplementary terms and symbols

Numerous terms and symbols supplement the rhythm and pitch notation in conveying the composer's intentions to performers. The terms are primarily descriptive words of Italian origin. The symbols transmit directions simply or graphically. Together they guide performers in matters of speed, loudness, style, mood, and repetition. Commonly used terms and symbols are introduced in the following pages. For a complete listing with definitions a dictionary, such as the *Pronouncing Pocket-Manual of Musical Terms* edited by Dr. Theodore Baker and published by G. Schirmer, is recommended.

✠    ✠    ✠    ✠

The *tempo* is the pace or rate of speed in music. The _____ is specified at the
TEMPO
beginning of most compositions in the native language of the country or in Italian, the universal language of music. The basic Italian tempo terms are listed in order from slow to fast with English equivalents:

*Largo* — broad, large, stately

*Lento* — slow

*Adagio* — slow, tranquil, at ease

*Andante* — moving, walking, going along

*Moderato* — moderate

*Allegro* — quick, cheerful, brisk, lively

*Presto* — rapid, very fast

The tempo terms, arranged from slow to fast in a row, are:

| Slow | | Fast |
| --- | --- | --- |

| Largo | Lento | Adagio | Andante | Moderato | Allegro | Presto |

Copy the tempo terms in reverse order from fast to slow.

| Fast | | Slow |
| --- | --- | --- |

| PRESTO | ALLEGRO | MODERATO | ANDANTE | ADAGIO | LENTO | LARGO |

Comparing the seven tempo terms which have been introduced:

*Allegro* is faster than *moderato* but slower than _____.
PRESTO

*Lento* is slower than *adagio* but faster than _____.
LARGO

A moderate tempo is indicated by the Italian word _____.
MODERATO

The tempo between *adagio* and *moderato* is _____.
ANDANTE

The fastest tempo indication is _____.
PRESTO

The slowest tempo indication is _____.
LARGO

The endings of the basic tempo terms are changed to modify their meanings as follows:

| A little slower | ←—Basic Term—→ | A little faster |
| --- | --- | --- |
| Larghissimo | Largo | Larghetto |
| Adagissimo | Adagio | Adagietto |
| Andantino* | Andante | Andantino* |
| Allegretto | Allegro | |
| | Presto | Prestissimo |

[*Note: Andantino *is interpreted both ways.*]

A *metronome* is a device for measuring tempos in terms of the number of beats per minute. A metronome mark at the beginning of a composition shows the note symbol of the beat and the number of beats per minute in this manner:

$$\text{♩} = 60$$

This metronome mark fixes the tempo at 60 quarter-note beats per minute.

What does this metronome mark mean?

$$\text{♪} = 120$$

_____ eighth-note beats per minute
120

Write a metronome mark for a tempo of 80 half-note beats per minute.

_____=_____
♩ = 80

*Ritardando (rit.)*, *rallentando (rall.)*, and *allargando (allarg.)* are terms which indicate a gradual decrease in the tempo or a holding back. This happens frequently at the end of compositions.

*Accelerando (accel.)*, similar to our word *accelerate*, means to increase the tempo gradually. *Stringendo (string.)* also indicates a gradual increase in the tempo and usually an increase in loudness at the same time.

✠     ✠     ✠     ✠

Soft and loud are indicated in music by the Italian words *piano* and *forte* or their abbreviations. *Piano* means soft. The name of the instrument originally was pianoforte, meaning that it could play soft and loud. The Italian word for loud is *forte*. The Italian word for soft is _____.
PIANO

*Forte* means _____.
LOUD

*Piano* and *forte* are usually abbreviated 𝒑 and 𝒇 . The abbreviation for *piano* is _____.
𝒑

The abbreviation for *forte* is _____. At the beginning of a passage which is to be
𝒇

loud, the letter _____ is written. *Piano* and *forte* are modified and the modifica-
𝒇

tions abbreviated as follows to provide six degrees of softness and loudness.

| Word | Abbreviation | Meaning |
|------|:---:|---------|
| *piano* | *p* | soft |
| *pianissimo* | *pp* | very soft, double piano |
| *mezzo piano* | *mp* | moderately soft |
| *forte* | *f* | loud |
| *fortissimo* | *ff* | very loud, double forte |
| *mezzo forte* | *mf* | moderately loud |

Write *louder* or *softer* between the pairs of abbreviations to give the correct meaning:

*f* is _____ LOUDER _____ than *p*

*p* is _____ SOFTER _____ than *f*

*pp* is _____ SOFTER _____ than *p*

*mp* is _____ LOUDER _____ than *p*

*mf* is _____ LOUDER _____ than *mp*

*mf* is _____ SOFTER _____ than *f*

*ff* is _____ LOUDER _____ than *f*

Write the abbreviations for the six dynamic levels in order from soft to loud.

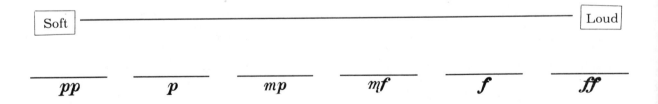

| Soft ———————————————————————— Loud |
|---|

*pp*  *p*  *mp*  *mf*  *f*  *ff*

The word meaning to increase the volume of sound gradually or to "get louder" is *crescendo*. *Crescendo* is abbreviated *cresc.*, sometimes *cres*. The sign for *crescendo* is two lines which start as a point and spread for the duration of the *crescendo*.

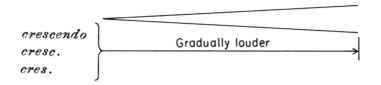

The opposite of *crescendo* is *decrescendo (decresc.* or *decres.)* or *diminuendo (dimin.* or *dim.).*
The *diminuendo* sign is the *crescendo* sign reversed.

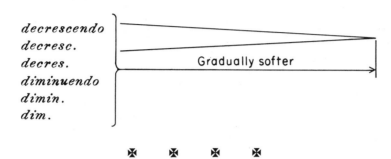

✠    ✠    ✠    ✠

Some of the following symbols and marks are found predominantly, others exclusively, in instrumental music.

Repeat Signs

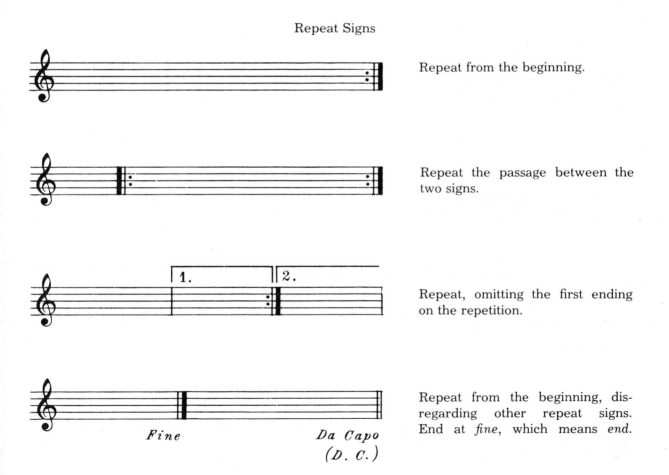

Repeat from the beginning.

Repeat the passage between the two signs.

Repeat, omitting the first ending on the repetition.

Repeat from the beginning, disregarding other repeat signs. End at *fine*, which means *end.*

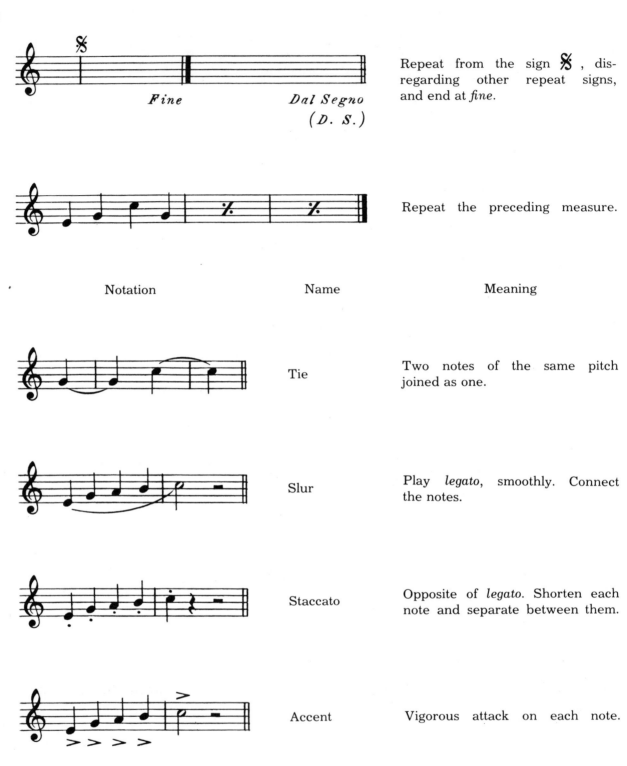

| Notation | Name | Meaning |
|---|---|---|
| | | Repeat from the sign 𝄋 , disregarding other repeat signs, and end at *fine*. |
| | | Repeat the preceding measure. |
| | Tie | Two notes of the same pitch joined as one. |
| | Slur | Play *legato*, smoothly. Connect the notes. |
| | Staccato | Opposite of *legato*. Shorten each note and separate between them. |
| | Accent | Vigorous attack on each note. |
| | Hold, Pause, or Fermata | Hold longer than the notated value. |

| Notation | Name | Meaning |
|---|---|---|
| | Grace Note | Small (grace) note played quickly just before the principal note. |
| | Trill | Alternate the written note and the note above it as fast as possible. |
| | Rolled (Arpeggiated) Chord | Play notes in rapid succession starting from the lowest. |
| | Pedal Mark | Depress piano sustaining pedal at *Ped.*, release at *. |
| | Pedal Mark | Apply piano sustaining pedal during sign. |

| Written | Called | Played |
|---|---|---|
| | Trill | |
| | Turn | |

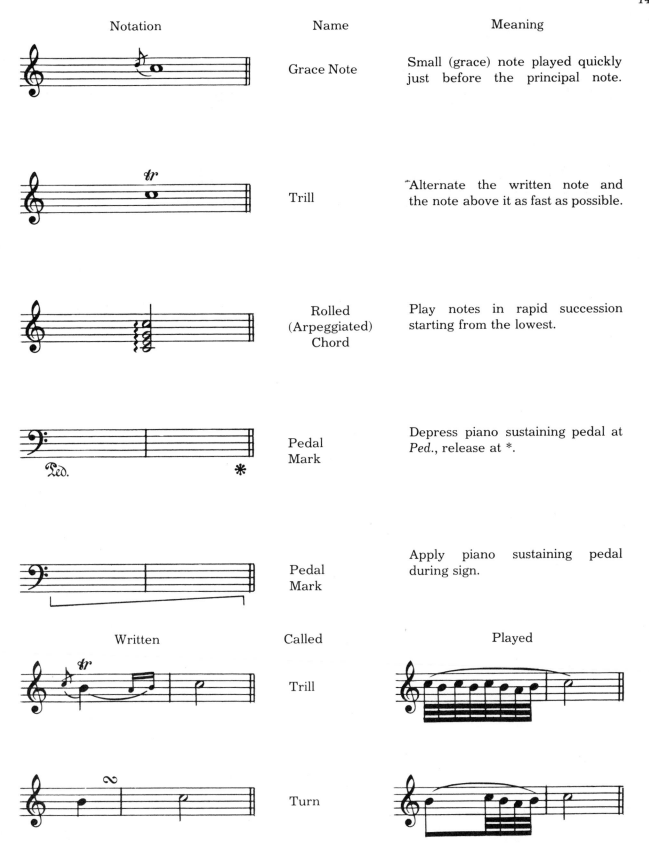

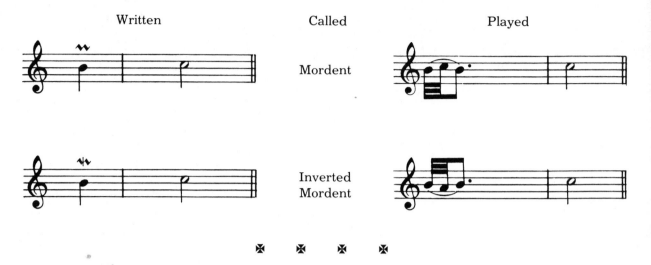

This completes your *Introduction to Music Reading.* You have taken a significant step in your musical development, and the knowledge and skills you have acquired will serve you well whatever your goals in music may be.

# index